KEYS to Marketing YOU to get THE JOB

Discover Your Potential. Become Essential.

AUTHORED BY

Dawn Ohaver Moyer | Jenny Casagrande

ISBN: 1495396185
ISBN 13: 9781495396182
Library of Congress Control Number: 2014902150
CreateSpace Independent Publishing Platform
North Charleston, South Carolina

For Maggie and Liz

ACKNOWLEDGMENTS

Thank you to our parents (Allan, Charles, Glenna, Marian and Rosann), Matt, Sarah, Kathy, Roshaunda, Mike and the Wonderful Women of Winston for your encouragement and support.

Thank you to Delta Phi Epsilon and our student network groups in the M100 class at Poole School of Management at North Carolina State University for your inspiration.

Thank you to Colleen, our editor, for guiding us to be better and better.

And finally, thank you to Nora, Otto, Ava, and Heidi for your unconditional love.

CONTENTS

Introduction

THE MAJORITY OF YOUR COURSEWORK IS behind you. Maybe you've done a summer internship, led leadership projects at school, moved away from home, or even started your first job.

Now what?

We are here to help you understand your *potential* and how you can become *essential* as you shape your career. We will show you how to use your skills and experiences to present yourself to prospective employers and create keys to unlock future success.

The authors of this book have pulled together a framework to help you get where you want to go. This framework is based on over twenty years of our marketing, market research, and sales experience in businesses from packaged goods to pharmaceuticals and from Fortune 500 companies to family-owned ventures. We've managed budgets in the millions of dollars and earned money for our employers in the billions of dollars.

In addition, we have mentored individuals just entering their careers to those making a "big" change. One common element continues to stand out: it's all about marketing! So we have taken our marketing expertise and applied it to the needs expressed by our mentees to develop a simple framework.

We founded Potential Essential, LLC with a mission to guide individuals to discover their inner *potential*, to become *essential* in the workplace, and to remain *key* to the organization. We are passionate about helping you to get to where you want to go and have developed the following objectives for this book:

1. Discover your *potential* and establish your *Essential Branding Statement*.
2. Determine your *Essential Demonstrated Behaviors*.
3. Articulate your value to hiring managers.

In order to understand your *potential* and what you have to offer, you need to understand yourself, including your needs, strengths, limitations, likes and dislikes, willingness to change, and inflexibilities. Basically, you need to learn a bit more about who you are and what you are about. It's also important for you to determine employers' needs, wants, and requirements. In other words, what do employers want and need from you and why? This process will allow you to match your *potential* with employers' needs and communicate with employers more effectively.

Definitions

Potential: having the capacity to become or develop into something in the future.

Essential: having an absolutely necessary capability or being absolutely necessary.

The following three steps will assist you in discovering and articulating your *potential* so you can become *essential* to get the job!

 Discovering your *potential*: exploring your strengths and values to establish your *Essential Branding Statement*

 Unlocking your *Essential Demonstrated Behaviors*: identifying your experiences/skills and how they translate to what companies are looking for in an employee

 Becoming *essential*: practicing effective communication of your *Essential Branding Statement* and *Essential Demonstrated Behaviors* in interviews, elevator pitches, cover letters, and resumes

All the steps we will share with you add up to pretty simple equations.

(Unique ID + Motivational Force + *Guide*) X Communication =
Essential Branding Statement

(Action Phrases + Relevant Experiences / Skills) X Behaviors =
Essential Demonstrated Behaviors

Essential Branding Statement + *Essential Demonstrated Behaviors* =
Success

Throughout this book we will provide you with examples of how these principles can be applied. We will follow the fictional character, "Cindy," throughout the book with specific examples that take her through the steps. We will also share examples of familiar brands and how, by using the same marketing principles large companies and brands use, you can market yourself to get *the job.*

Definition

Elevator pitch: a concise, memorable introduction (as if you only have the time it takes for an elevator to travel from the twelfth floor to the lobby). It can be used in a variety of situations, including career fairs.

one

Discovering Your *Potential* to Establish Your *Essential Branding Statement*

OUR LIVES ARE FULL OF ALL kinds of keys: keys that unlock our homes, cars, apartments, lockers, bike locks. There are key cards to get into buildings and hotel rooms. Even credit cards are kinds of keys that allow access to money and purchases. Keys open the puzzles, locks, and restraints in our lives when we need to reach a goal or milestone.

We are helping you create a key, your *Essential Branding Statement*, that will help unlock possibilities for you as you graduate from college and/or begin to find a path toward a career for yourself.

Keys, no matter what the form, are made up of some distinct parts that work together. For us, the term "key" makes us think of an old-fashioned skeleton key. A skeleton key has three parts: a bit, a shank, and a bow.

Defining the *Key* for *Essential Branding Statement*

Bit: the front part of a key, which has teeth or grooves. The uniqueness of the bit allows for specific use in specific locks.

Bow: the flat back end of a key the user grips to twist and lock or unlock.

Shank: the straight narrow part of a key that connects the bow with the bit.

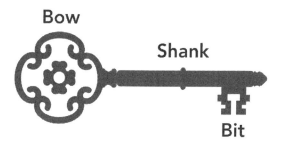

Each part has a unique function that, when working together with the other parts, creates a marvelous working key that's unique to you and designed to take you where you want to go. Our version of the skeleton key works like this:

- The bit, or what we call the ***Unique ID***, includes
  - » Your **core values** are **the foundation** of short-term goals and long-term career fulfillment.
  - » Knowing your **strengths** will allow you to match who you are with what you do.

- The bow, or what we call ***Motivational Force***, is the end of the key that allows you to activate the force you need to turn your key.
  - » Understanding the values and higher purpose that **motivates and inspires you** will provide a path forward.
- The shank, or what we call the ***Guide***, connects the bit and bow of a key. In this case, it connects your ***Unique ID*** and ***Motivational Force***.
  - » The ***Guide*** uses your ***Motivational Force*** and ***Unique ID*** to provide you with a **working plan** and a measure to assist with decision making.

All of these components determine your *Essential Branding Statement*, enabling you to communicate your passions, skills, and strengths in a way that draws hiring managers and companies to you. Your brand enables others to understand you and what makes you different and memorable. Using this method of building a branding statement will allow you to achieve your goals and align opportunities with your values and skills.

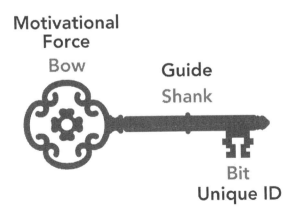

Definition

Essential Branding Statement: this is the **benefits and features you offer,** articulated for a hiring manager/company.

For example, if we look at the credit card market, there are four key players: MasterCard, Visa, Discover, and American Express. Each one fundamentally works the same and is issued to a specific person(s) or group as a method of payment. They all allow the cardholder to pay for goods and/or services based on the holders' promise to repay their balance, and in turn, the card companies charge the cardholder a fee and/or interest on the purchases. The services are remarkably similar in a very competitive and crowded market. You can obtain a card through a bank, a store, or an organization. Many have customized features and benefits to the specific customer to whom they are targeting. They may offer some of the following:

- Low Interest
- Balance Transfers
- Zero percent APR
- Rewards (Points, Gas Cards, Store Credit)
- Cash Back
- Travel & Airline Perks
- No Foreign Transaction Fees
- Cards for Business
- Cards for Students
- Prepaid & Debit Cards
- Instant Approval Offers

Let's look at three examples of how these companies market themselves to different target customers by communicating how the particular card can meet their specific needs. These examples will show you how credit card companies are sharing their *potential* and becoming *essential* to their customer.

US AIRWAYS DIVIDEND MILES MASTERCARD BY BARCLAYS BANK DELAWARE[1]

Message: Miles of Possibilities: Bonjour earn up to 40,000 bonus miles
Target Customer: Frequent personal and business travelers

Benefits include:
- Redeem flights for 5,000 fewer miles
- Earn 2 miles for every $1 you spend in purchases and 1 mile for every $1 you spend everywhere else
- Annual companion ticket good for up to 2 companion tickets at $99 each, plus taxes and fees
- Zone 2 boarding and First Class check-in

AMERICAN EXPRESS BUSINESS CARD[2]

Message: Power to Purchase. Power to Earn.
Target Customer: Small to medium business owners

Benefits include:
- Earn 3x the points on airfare purchased directly from airlines and 2x the points on US purchases for advertising in select media. Shipping and at gas stations.
- Purchasing power for your business: Enhanced Business Gold Rewards Card gives you spending power that can grow as your business grows.

    Simplify the way you manage expenses: upload receipts with the ReceiptMatchSM mobile app, by email, or from your online statement.

BANANA REPUBLIC VISA CARD[3]

Message: Rewards Are Always in Style.
Target Customer: Young professional men and women

Benefits include:

- Earn 15% off the entire first purchase at Banana Republic
- Earn rewards with purchase
- Card member only offers, promotions, and discounts

In each of these examples, the credit card company positions what it has to offer the customer group by developing *key* messages with benefits that resonate with that customer. Even though this is a crowded market with products of similar offerings, each credit card finds a way to differentiate themselves from the others using their benefits, features, and *potential*.

Over the next few chapters, we will help you begin to develop your *essential* brand so you can differentiate yourself and get *the job* you want!

two

Defining Your Unique ID

LET'S GET STARTED CREATING YOUR *ESSENTIAL Branding Statement.*

Unique ID includes

- **Core values: the foundation of everything** moving forward and *key* to short- and long-term career fulfillment
- **Strengths:** defining these will allow you to match who you are with what you do

Definitions

Core Values: concepts, principles, or standards that drive one's decisions and actions.

Strengths: inherent ability to do something.

Unique ID: Understanding Your Core Values

The first step in creating your *Unique ID* is getting clear on who you are and what you are about, otherwise known as...identifying your core values.

A core value is important in understanding how you relate to people. Sometimes values are not obvious on the surface of interactions with others but lie underneath the words in a conversation.

In addition to being the concepts, principles, or standards that drive one's decisions and actions, core values also offer an insight into who you are and what you believe in.

Examples: trust, friendship, hard work, success

Definition

Insight: to gain an accurate and deep intuitive understanding of yourself.

Values may change slightly in priority over time as you grow personally and professionally. It's always good to go back and revisit them prior to assessing major life decisions.

For example, financial reward may be at the top of your list of things that are important to you when you're in your twenties, but family may become more of a core value later in life. However, for the most part, in our experience, your core value themes tend to stay the same. They might just move up or down in rank.

When determining your core values, there are a few questions to ask yourself.

1. How do you aspire to live your life?
2. What would you fight for? (And why?)
3. During a time of conflict with a person or organization, what did I feel was at the core of the disagreement?

 CINDY'S EXAMPLE

Cindy just graduated from college with a bachelor's of science in finance and accounting management degree and took an entry-level job as a financial analyst in a large corporation. Her job responsibilities include:

- Reviewing performance and analysis
- Providing portfolio and asset analytics as requested by the investment managers
- Quality checks on valuation, performance, and transaction data
- Manual performance calculations when requested
- Creating daily, monthly, and quarterly reports
- Reconciliation of daily accounts as needed

Cindy identified her core values to be collaboration, family, positivity, creativity, and freethinking.

Let's start with a values exercise to assist you in determining your core values.

The appendix includes a list of different values. None are right or wrong, "good" or "bad." Consider the questions above and cross out the words in the list of values that *don't* resonate with you. Next, take the shortened list and narrow them down further to no more than five core values. Finally, list them below in ranking order of importance to you. This may take some time, but once you have the pieces in place, you will be well on your way to building your story to convey your *potential*.

INSERT YOUR TOP THREE TO FIVE CORE VALUES HERE.

1. _____

2. _____

3. _____

4. _____

5. _____

You can also fill these core values into the **Summary *Key*** in the appendix

Unique ID: Understanding Your *Key* Strengths

The second step to creating your *Unique ID* involves understanding your strengths.

Strengths are not just things like getting an A in math or scoring the most points in a game. They're also about how you feel when you're doing something. When you feel energized when you're doing an activity or skill, it's a natural strength for you. The opposite is true when you think about doing something that is not a strength: it makes you exhausted, drained, or you dread doing the activity.

Understanding strengths is important because it will help you understand

- The value you can offer to a company or job
- How you would fit in at a company and/or particular role in a company
- Where you will find and gain positive energy when you work

 CINDY'S EXAMPLE

Cindy is highly creative and strategic, as well as a positive thinker. However, she took a job that was all spreadsheets and numbers. She was exhausted, miserable, and dissatisfied with her job. A financial analyst job was not for her...but a financial strategy role might be better! This would allow Cindy to use her creativity to solve financial questions and be a strategic partner to her clients.

Ways to Identify and Understand Your *Key* Strengths

1. Ask five different people your strengths. List the key words they use.
2. Think about your fantasy job and ask yourself what you like about imagining yourself in that role and what you like about the role itself. Add those to your list.
3. Create a word cloud like those found on www.wordle.net from your resume or a description of a past activity/job that you enjoyed, and select key words that resonate with you.

 NOTE

Some people can list a thousand goods things about themselves and some people can't think of one! Work with friends, family, teachers, and/or mentors to identify the list. Or if you find you're still struggling, pretend you are writing a list of strengths for someone else. This can give you the freedom or permission to think about yourself differently. Before you finalize your strengths, check in with your with friends, family, teachers, and/or mentors to get a second opinion.

The appendix includes a list of some common strengths. This is not an exhaustive list but can be used as a guide to get you started.

INSERT YOUR TOP FIVE TO TEN STRENGTHS HERE.

1. _Honesty, Optimism, Innovation,_
2. _Public speaking, perseverence,_
3. _Leadership, planning_
4. _____
5. _____
6. _____
7. _____
8. _____
9. _____
10. _____

Now that you have created your list of *key* strengths, take some time to look for commonalities. Wherever possible, group strengths that are relevant to your career interests or the type of work you consider meaningful to you. You're looking for themes.

CINDY'S EXAMPLE

After getting feedback from her friends and people she worked with, Cindy's strengths list looked like this.

- Different ways to say things
- Good with big picture
- Lots of ideas
- Photography
- Lots of energy
- Positive
- Works well in a group
- Strong written and verbal skills

- Gets the job done
- Outgoing
- Inspires others
- Charity work
- Sees different perspectives
- Planner
- Goal oriented

From this list there are strengths that can be placed together into groupings. It's best to pair groupings down to three to five themes that best represent who you are and where you want to go. Based on Cindy's strengths and career interests, we selected the following groupings: Creative, Team player, Positive, Results oriented and Strategic thinker.

GROUPS OF SIMILAR STRENGTHS	GROUPINGS
Different ways to say things Lots of ideas Photography	Creative
Lots of energy Positive Works well in a group Outgoing Inspires others Charity work	Team player
Good with big picture Sees different perspectives Planner	Strategic thinker
Lots of energy Works well in a group Inspires others Charity work	Positive
Gets the job done Planner Goal oriented	Results oriented
Strong written and verbal skills	Communication skills

Place your strengths into groupings, and then select your top three to five strengths. We will use this list of strengths to continue to develop your *Essential Branding Statement.*

GROUPS OF SIMILAR STRENGTHS	GROUPINGS

ENTER TOP THREE TO FIVE *KEY* STRENGTHS GROUPED.

1. _____

2. _____

3. _____

4. _____

5. _____

If you want to dive deeper into your *key* strengths, there is more information on how to do this in the appendix. There is also a ***Summary Key*** available to capture your strengths.

three

Core Values & Strengths

Now that you understand your core values and *key* strengths, we will build on them to create your *Motivational Force*.

Understanding Your *Motivational Force*

Motivational Force: the end of the key that allows you to activate the force you need to turn your key. Why is it important to understand your *Motivational Force*? Because it can assist you with the decision making process. Every time you need to make a decision, you can look back at it and see if you're on track…if it "fits" with what drives you each and every day.

Your *Motivational Force* should be personal. It should inspire and motivate you to reach your goals. It will help you evaluate potential jobs and life-changing career events like working in a new area, moving for a job, or taking less pay to gain more experience.

 EXAMPLE

Matt wanted to be a teacher, so in the summer he worked as an aide for a nursery school even though it paid less than a job waiting tables. This gave him valuable experience to showcase when he went to apply for internships his junior year.

Without understanding *Motivational Force*, you are in danger of just going through the motions and trying to survive by making short-sighted decisions. This can lead to never feeling fulfilled or satisfied on your career journey.

In more practical terms, it also gives you direction or discussion points in an interview or informal conversation with a key influencer who asks you what you want to do and why. You will always be ready!

Definition

Key Influencer: a person who has the power to cause change or affect someone's opinion.

It's OK that your *Motivational Force* will probably change as your evolve over time and gain new experiences. For now let's focus on setting a direction for what's next. This process will help you to set short-term goals and shape long-term direction. Now is the time to start thinking in a "bigger picture" or an overall stretch of where you want to be and who you want to be in the future.

Let's look at a few companies and how they use *Motivational Force* as they aspire to set strategies and motivate employees.

 NOTE

Motivational Force is similar to a vision statement for corporations. However, we have chosen this language to better represent how it is used and to simplify the concept.

AMAZON[4]

"Our vision is to be Earth's most customer centric company; to build a place where people can come to find and discover anything they might want to buy online."

FACEBOOK[5]

"People use Facebook to stay connected with friends and family, to discover what's going on in the world, and to share and express what matters to them."

 CINDY'S EXAMPLE

If we look at Cindy's core values and career motivation, here's what her *Motivational Force* might look like.

To use my ability to design creative financial strategies and positivity to enable a world where people can enjoy life as it is now and be confident about the future.

Creating Your Own *Motivational Force*

To help you create your *Motivational Force* below are a few writing tips and examples.

Writing Tips

- Write in first person.
- Limit to about fifty words.
- Be clear and memorable.
- Use your own words. It's great to get input from others, but the statement itself should be from your heart. You need to believe it in order to use it!
- It should be inspirational and visionary yet realistic...a stretch but not completely, freakishly impossible.

Below are some additional examples for different types of careers:

ADDITIONAL EXAMPLES OF MOTIVATIONAL FORCE STATEMENTS

TEACHER

I want to use my natural passion for teaching others to educate children to be the best they can be. My belief is that every child deserves a chance and can learn.

RETAIL MANAGEMENT

My vision is to run one of the largest clothing retail chains by using my leadership skill, love of fashion, and passion for customer service. I believe if you listen and serve the customer you can help them obtain the look and image they want.

IT / COMPUTER SERVICES

I imagine being part of a high-tech business and running at the speed of light to ensure that employees can be efficient and more productive. I want to use my talent for creatively solving IT problems to enable a stress-free IT world.

Insert your *Motivational Force* statement below. You can also add it into the **Summary *Key*** in the appendix.

---

four

Creating Your *Guide*

CREATING A *GUIDE* (THE SHANK OF the key) works with your *Motivational Force* and *Unique ID* to provide you with a working plan and a measure to assist with decision-making. A *Guide* will build on your *Unique ID* and use your *Motivational Force* to develop a strategy to live your values and attain your goals. If you are *not* clear on your own *Guide*, your future may be shaped or influenced by others and society (in a bad way). So take the time now, and invest in your *potential*!

NOTE

A *Guide* is similar to a mission statement for corporations. However, we have chosen this manner of speaking to better represent how it is used and simplify the concept.

Let's check back now to see how Amazon's and Facebook's *Guide* fits with their *Motivational Force*.

AMAZON

Motivational Force:[4] "Our vision is to be Earth's most customer centric company; to build a place where people can come to find and discover anything they might want to buy online."

Guide:[6] "We seek to be Earth's most customer-centric company for four primary customer sets: consumers, sellers, enterprises, and content creators."

FACEBOOK

Motivational Force:[5] "People use Facebook to stay connected with friends and family, to discover what's going on in the world, and to share and express what matters to them."

Guide:[5] "Facebook's mission is to give people the power to share and make the world more open and connected."

Both companies use their *Motivational Force* to inspire and create a vision for the future, and then they add the *Guide* so it's clear to all that interact with them (internal and external) what they stand for and how they want to achieve their goals.

MOTIVATIONAL FORCE

I want to use my creative ability to design financial strategies. I want to use positive thinking to enable a world where people can enjoy life now and be confident about the future.

GUIDE

I want to become a leader in financial strategy at a midsize company. I will do this by understanding my clients' needs, developing creative solutions, and designing programs to keep them motivated and encouraged to save for the future.

Here are the corresponding *Guides* that build on the *Motivational Force* examples for different types of careers:

ADDITIONAL EXAMPLES OF *MOTIVATIONAL FORCE* STATEMENTS

TEACHER

Motivational Force: I want to use my natural passion for teaching others to educate children to be the best they can be. My belief is that every child deserves a chance and can learn.

Guide: I want to become a grade school teacher so that I can educate and develop children early in their formative years. I will do this by finding creative ways to reach children, spark their imagination, and create a safe learning environment.

RETAIL MANAGEMENT

Motivational Force: My vision is to run one of the largest clothing retail chains by using my leadership skill, love of fashion, and passion for customer service. I believe that if you listen and serve the customer, you can help them obtain the look and image they want.

Guide: I want to be known by my customers as someone who is committed to providing them with quality fashion advice and exceptional customer service. I will lead my company and be known by my peers as someone who is a team player, learner, and solution seeker.

IT / COMPUTER SERVICES

Motivational Force: I imagine being part of a high-tech business running at the speed of light to ensure that employees can be efficient and more productive. I want to use my talent for creatively solving IT problems to enable a stress-free IT world.

Guide: I want to provide innovative solutions to create practical stress-free IT solutions by looking for ways to increase efficiencies and to increase customer satisfaction.

....

CREATING YOUR OWN *GUIDE*

The following are writing tips and examples to help you create your personal *Guide*.

Writing tips

- Write in first person.
- Be simple, clear, and concise.
- Try to limit to two to four sentences.
- Answer how you want to achieve your goals.
- Frame the statements positively.
- Make them both compelling to others and a guide for you.

Below are a few template sentences to get you started. Fill in the brackets and begin creating your own personal *Guide*. You can use them together or combine bits and pieces as you like to form your own.[7]

- "To [what you want to achieve, do, or become] so that [phrases from *Motivational Force*]. I will do this by [*key strengths*]."
- "I value [core values] because [phrases from *Motivational Force*]. Accordingly, I will [what you can do to live by these core values]."
- "To live each day with [phrases from *Motivational Force*], I will do [desired result] by [specific behaviors or *key strengths*]."

- "To be known by [an important person/group to you] as someone who is [strengths or phrase from *Motivational Force*] to achieve [desired result]."

Insert your *Guide* below. You can also add it into the **Summary *Key*** in the appendix.

_____

_____

_____

_____

five

Essential Branding

NOW THAT YOU HAVE COMPLETED the three parts of the *essential* key, we can put the parts of the key together and create your *Essential Branding Statement.*

(Unique ID + Motivational Force + *Guide*) X Communication = *Essential Branding Statement*

In this fast-paced, ever-changing, and competitive world we live in, in order to stand out from the crowd of resumes, online posts, first interviews, and informational interactions, you need to grow your brand. Personal branding consists of many facets including how you look, act, and communicate. Iconic brands are built by understanding the customers' need and the ability to deliver the customers' need in a unique way. Not only will your brand need to resonate with your potential employer, but you will continue to grow your brand over time. If you think about an established brand (e.g., Coke or McDonald's), you have certain expectations of what you will receive when you interact with that brand. The same is true about your *essential* brand. You want people to associate you and your work with the brand you have created. It's important to understand how to create your *essential* brand and avoid unintentionally creating a brand that doesn't accurately represent who you are or what you want to stand for.

In this section of the book, we explore how to create your *Essential Branding Statement*. Then we'll review how to communicate your brand so you can differentiate yourself, be clear on what value you bring to an organization, and ensure that when the right opportunity comes up, you are at the top of your audience's mind.

When a brand resonates with the customer, it starts the process of being the "product of choice." We want you to become the "candidate of choice" for your next opportunity.

Definitions

Iconic brands have a strong identity and become more or less cultural icons.

Product of choice is the brand or version of a product that is preferred by the target customer group (e.g. Coke vs. Pepsi or Ford vs. Mazda).

Iconic brands include Apple, McDonald's, and Target. All of these brands have very distinctive looks, clear messages and communicate how they deliver customers' needs in a way that separates them from their competition, even when they offer similar products.

We recognize that, just like brands such as IBM, Ford, and even 007 (James Bond), there might be a time where you will need to shift your branding or update your image. We will address these situations in another book.

Let's begin by developing your *Essential Branding Statement*, which includes elements from the key (*Unique IDs, Motivational Force*, and your *Guide*) so that you can communicate this information in a convenient and concise way to a prospective employer.

In general, unless you're theorizing about your vocation or directly asked about where you see yourself in a fantasy future, you would not articulate your *Motivational Force* or *Guide* word-for-word. We will build your *Essential Branding Statement* to deliver this information because its designed to take into account the way an employer or customer needs to hear what you have to say.

Let's extend examples of two companies we discussed earlier (McDonald's and Target) further.

MCDONALD'S MISSION STATEMENT[8]

Our goal is becoming customers' favorite way and place to eat and drink by serving core favorites.

MCDONALD'S KEY MESSAGE[8]

I'm lovin' it.

TARGET'S MISSION STATEMENT[9]

Our mission is to make Target your preferred shopping destination in all channels by delivering outstanding value, continuous innovation, and exceptional guest experiences by consistently fulfilling our Expect More. Pay Less.' brand promise.

TARGET'S KEY MESSAGE[9]

Expect more. Pay less.

In these two examples, they have taken their vision and mission statements and translated them into a message that will resonate with their customers. If they just advertised with their vision or mission statement, it would not be memorable and would fall flat on most customers. That's why, just like with companies or products, it's better to develop an *essential* brand you can own and that employers will see as relevant and memorable.

Building Your *Essential Branding Statement*

Return to your *key* strengths and choose three that you feel are ones you want to communicate to as part of your brand.

Tips on how to select your top three strengths

- Determine skills and/or experiences that are considered important for your area of interest (look at web postings, company websites, expert blogs, and articles written about the industry or company for points of reference).
- Consider what complementary strengths would set you apart from other candidates.
- Look for areas that were strong themes. For example, if you said you were a team player but no one else identified this as strength for you, it may not resonate with your employer.

- Ask academic advisors, mentors, or colleagues from internships or other work.

CINDY'S EXAMPLE

Cindy selected Creative, Team player, Positivity, Results oriented and Strategic thinker as her five *key* strengths. We will use Creative, Strategic thinker, and Positivity as her *key* strengths. These align with the direction she wants her career to go *and* are unique to her.

ENTER YOUR TOP THREE *KEY* STRENGTHS.

1. _____

2. _____

3. _____

You can also fill these top three strengths into the **Summary *Key*** in the appendix.

There are several ways to articulate your strengths in a statement to make them "come to life" as you communicate them. Using action verbs is one way to express your strengths and articulate the value of the strength. In the appendix are a few action verbs to consider.

Once you have determined your top three *key* strengths, write a strength statement about each one of them. A strength statement will support your *essential* brand. In other words, these strength statements are the "proof" or facts underlying your *Essential Branding Statement.* The strength statements should reflect the three strengths you've identified as relevant and that you can clearly communicate an outcome of having and using that strength. These statements will be part of the tools (cover letters, interviews, email communications, etc.) we will discuss later to effectively communicate your *essential* brand.

BELOW ARE A FEW TEMPLATE PHRASES TO GET YOU STARTED.

1. The ability [insert strength] to [insert action verb]
2. [Insert strength] who can [insert action verb]
3. [Insert strength] that enables me [insert action verb]

 CINDY'S EXAMPLE

Based on Cindy's *Motivational Force, Guide,* and *key* strengths, here are three possible strength statements.

1. Ability to identify creative solutions based on customer needs
2. Strategic thinker who can deliver on short- and long-term goals
3. Positive viewpoint that enables me to motivate others to reach their goals

ENTER YOUR TOP THREE *KEY* STRENGTHS USING A STRENGTH STATEMENT FORMAT.

1. ....

_____

2. ....

_____

3. ....

_____

Now that we have these, what do we do with them? We will start by creating a memorable statement of who you are and why you are the "candidate of choice" with your *key* strength statement as support. We will assist you in creating a powerful and engaging statement designed to articulate your value in a way your prospective employer needs to hear it and begin to create how the professional world knows you.

Things to consider when developing your *Essential Branding Statement* are as follows:

- How will people recognize your brand, your uniqueness?
- What will stand out?
- Are your words memorable, yet sound like you?
- What do you want to hear back about yourself if someone else were saying this information?
- Does it include any of your *Guide* or *Motivational Force* elements?
- Is it clear and concise?

Branding Statement Templates

1. I use my [insert a strength or strengths] to [insert what you do] for [target audience] so that they [insert they will do] to get [insert result(s)].
2. To obtain [insert result] for [target audience], I have the ability to [insert strengths] to [insert result] because I am motivated by [insert piece of your *Motivational Force* or *Guide*].
3. I [insert what you do at work] by using my natural abilities of [insert strengths] to achieve [insert desired result].

 CINDY'S *ESSENTIAL BRANDING STATEMENT*

Based on Cindy's *Motivational Force, Guide,* and *key* strengths, here is how the components of her *Essential Branding Statement* might build to a statement:

Motivational Force: I will use my creative ability to design financial strategies and positive thinking to enable a world where people can enjoy life now and be confident about the future.

Guide: In order to become a leader in financial strategy at a midsize company, I will understand my clients' needs, develop creative solutions, and design programs to keep them motivated and encouraged to save for the future.

Key Strengths: Creative, Strategic thinker, and Positivity

Essential Branding Statement: I use my ability to think strategically combined with my creativity to design financial planning solutions to allow people to enjoy life now and keep them motivated to save for the future.

Here are *Essential Branding Statements* that build on the corresponding *Guides* and *Motivational Force* examples for different types of careers:

ADDITIONAL EXAMPLES OF ESSENTIAL BRANDING STATEMENTS

TEACHER

Motivational Force: I want to use my natural passion for teaching others to educate children to be the best they can be. My belief is that every child deserves a chance and can learn.

Guide: I want to become a grade school teacher so that I can educate and develop children early in their formative years. I will do this by finding creative ways to reach children, spark their imagination, and create a safe learning environment.

Essential Branding Statement: I use my passion for teaching to develop children so that they will be the best they can be by developing creative ways to reach children, sparking their imagination, and creating a safe learning environment.

RETAIL MANAGEMENT

Motivational Force: My vision is to run one of the largest retail clothing chains by using my leadership skills, love of fashion, and passion for customer service. I believe that if you listen and serve the customer, you can help them obtain the look and image they want.

Guide: I want to be known by my customers as someone who is committed to providing them with quality fashion advice and exceptional customer service. I want to be known by my company as a leader among my peers and as someone who is a team player, learner, and solution oriented worker.

Essential Branding Statement: I have the ability to provide superb fashion advice and exceptional customer service to assist the customer in obtaining the look and image they want and increase profits for the company. I do this by identifying the customer's need and aligning it to solutions offered by the company.

IT/COMPUTER SOLUTIONS

Motivational Force: I imagine being part of a high-tech business, running at the speed of light, and ensuring that employees can be efficient and more productive. I want to use my talent for creatively solving IT problems to enable a stress-free IT world.

Guide: I want to live each day learning new things and providing innovative solutions to create practical, stress-free IT solutions. I will do this by looking for ways to increase IT efficiencies to increase customer profitability and satisfaction.

Essential Branding Statement: Because I am motivated by increasing IT efficiencies to improve customer profitability and satisfaction, I provide company employees with innovative IT solutions by using my strong technical skills combined with strategic thinking.

....

INSERT YOUR *ESSENTIAL BRANDING STATEMENT* BELOW.

Because I enjoy enriching others, I
~~leadership,~~
~~use~~ use my planning and organization
skills to ~~coordinate &~~ fun and exciting events.
coordinate &   & educational
facilitate

Testing Your *Essential Branding Statement*

Share your *Essential Branding Statement* with a few friends, family, or advisors, and see what they take away from your statement. If it's not what you intended, consider what caused the disconnect.

Let's take Dawn, for example. At one point in her career, she shared with her management team that she had "a passion for developing people." This led several leaders in the company to think that she wanted to join the human resources department or become a sales leader when in fact neither of those roles laddered up to her *Motivational Force* or measured very well with her *Guide*. She had not completed the *Essential Branding Statement*. The concept of "developing" was how she did what she did (a strength) but not what she did (a result). So she regrouped and created a more impactful statement, painting a clearer picture of who she was, where she wanted to go, and why she was the "candidate of choice" for the roles she was interested in.

How to Make an *Essential Branding Statement* Work for You

Once you have a strong *Essential Branding Statement,* you can tailor your specific message to the opportunity. This can be done by understanding what the company and/or interviewer is looking for and how your *essential* brand can meet those needs. The need of the hiring manager can differ by opportunity or company and still align with your *essential* brand. We will explore more deeply into this topic in the "Pulling It All Together" chapter of this book.

You can now add your *Essential Branding Statement* in to the **Summary Key** in the appendix!

six

Looking for a Job

Develop a Job Search Plan

WE SUGGEST CREATING A SPREADSHEET OR other way to organize your goals, track your progress, and evaluate what's working and what's not.

There are several ways to go about looking for a job. We are going to list a few of them and you may want to include them in your personal job search plan:

- Networking (building your professional community)
- Job search engines (e.g., www.careerbuilder.com, www.monster.com)
- Job posting boards (e.g., www.indeed.com, www.simplyhired.com)
- Professional online networks (e.g., LinkedIn.com)
- Job fairs (school or community)
- Job search groups
- Career center job listings or campus interview boards
- Trade or professional associations
- Trade or professional associations newsletters

- Newspaper classified ads (most major cities are online)
- Employment services and agencies run by both government and for-profit businesses
- Company of interest job posting
- Local Chamber of Commerce in areas you are interested in living

Many jobs are not advertised and can only be discovered through engaging with companies and individuals in your field of interest. We strongly suggest you use a few of these methods in your search for a job and include them in your job search plan. Below are a few ideas:

- Proactively send a letter of interest and your resume to the human resources department and specific managers of organizations you might be interested in. The success of this method is greatly increased when you follow up by sending letters, emails or make phone calls to inquire about potential job openings or to schedule an informational interview.
- Register with a few recruitment agencies that specialize in your area of interest and in general entry-level positions.
- Look for areas to volunteer and meet others that have similar interests.
- Attend local seminars or association conferences in areas of interest.
- Contact the national headquarters of your sorority or fraternity.
- Join an organization of your field of interest.
- Contact your career development office at your school.
- Join local job seeker groups.
- Join a temporary employment agency.
- Do an internship or co-op with a company in your field.

- Use online professional networks to reach out to people in your field of interest.
- Engage your professional community (see next section for more information).

Building Your Professional Community

A few words about "networking": the idea can bring chills to many individuals, and it can be done awkwardly or brilliantly. If there is one skill that will move you forward faster or connect you to your dream job faster, "networking" is it. We prefer to look at it as building a professional community, similar to a social media tool, but deeper. (In the next book, we will go into more detail about people that influence and mentor you.) While we would like to say that doing a great job and working hard will automatically provide you with rewards like the next promotion or even a new opportunity, it rarely works this way.

A recent college graduate who excelled at school, had extracurricular activities, and two internships will still have to build relationships and leverage them. (Too often we see individuals that have relationships but don't know how to leverage them.) If you wait until you need a job, this can be too late or delay achievement of your goals. In order to be successful at building business relationships and contacts, you need to be authentic, interested in the other person, and offer them value in return (just like any relationship).

People to Consider in Your Community

- Relatives (especially those in similar fields)
- Friends of the family in your field of interest
- Recent graduates of your school
- Colleagues, advisors, and coaches you have meet in extracurricular activities
- Mentors and academic advisors
- Colleagues from internships, co-ops, and early jobs
- Members of organizations to which you belong
- Alumnae of your sorority or fraternity
- Individuals in roles you aspire to be in

There are a few different ways to build and stay in touch with your professional community. Below are a few suggestions:

- Create a professional account profile (e.g., LinkedIn).
- Send out articles of interest.
- E-mail others to congratulate them on a success.
- Update others on your progress and ask for advice.
- Leverage your community in reverse! For example, if you hear that a professional connection is having a difficult time accessing a new account and that account happens to be related to the mother of your soccer teammate, offer to introduce them.

Follow up from previous conversations. This is a key time for you to pay it forward. If your connection mentions something of interest, like a restaurant for example, and you just read an article about the best new restaurant in town, let them know!

Leverage Your Professional Community

- Ask for informational interviews.
- Ask to shadow an individual for the day to see what the job entails.
- Ask for referrals. Who do they know in your area of interest that they could introduce you to or speak on your behalf?
- Seek their advice on your resume.
- Connect via your social media, but don't forget the personal touch as well (having a cup of coffee can go a long way).

Definition

Informational interviews: appointments to talk with people who are currently working in the field to gain a better understanding of a career or industry and to build a network of contacts in that field.

Tips on requesting informational interviews:

- Request an appointment to discuss information you have obtained by reading annual reports, trade literature, and articles related to your field of interest, recent company announcements, or key decisions they have recently made. For example: "I understand Company X is planning to expand. I am completing an accounting degree and am very interested in understanding the implications to your global market. May I have twenty minutes of your time to discuss it?"

 Indicate your desire to meet with them, even if they have no positions currently available in their department. Some people find it useful to state that they will be looking for jobs in the near future but are now just gathering information about organizations or industries. *Do not* expect to be interviewed for a job at this juncture, but *do* determine ahead of time how to discuss your *essential* brand with them.

Remember that it's important for you to connect with the person and understand his or her needs. Take an interest in them, find ways you can help them and look for ways to continue to connect after the initial meeting. Out of those relationships come opportunities!

> ## 📋 *NOTE*
>
> *Always follow up* and *send a thank you note* (e-mail or hand written). Often the people you are seeking are super busy people that have made time to help you. Make sure you thank them, and let them know the outcome of the conversation. We can't tell you how many times people early in their career have asked for our help and either never followed up or thanked us until they required assistance the next time. If you get this opportunity, be sure to let the person you've met with know what happened. We would like to know!

seven

Understanding the Importance of Demonstrated Behaviors

How Do You Become the *Essential* Candidate with Most *Potential* to Offer?

So now that you've identified your *potential* and established your *Essential Branding Statement*, we need to understand the best way to articulate your value in a way a person hiring needs to hear it.

(Action Phrases + Relevant Experiences / Skills) X Behaviors =
Essential Demonstrated Behaviors

 Not only are employers looking for your skills, strengths, and experiences but also how you go about achieving your goals (behaviors). You may be surprised by the skills you have acquired. You may be unintentionally limiting your next steps because you don't know how to go about describing the way you achieve goals. We are not implying that you should exaggerate or make up skills or experiences you don't have. However, we have seen multiple examples of resumes and interviews (real and practice) in which skills and/or experiences have not been used to reflect the true knowledge gained and the behavior that was used to achieve goals.

Different resources refer to this as different things such as performance behaviors, leadership behaviors, or behavioral interviewing. We think of these resources as *Essential Demonstrated Behaviors*, and there are eight areas that can prepare you for anything from informal discussions to formal interviews to articulate why you are the candidate of choice.

 NOTE

This doesn't mean *all* these behaviors must be displayed or are relevant to a particular career or job. Some have a similar or interlocking "feel" about them. We'll talk more about how to assess which fit you, your experiences, and/or the behaviors an employer may be looking for.

In this section we will explore how to build your *Essential Demonstrated Behaviors* with the following:

- Identify relevant experiences and skills.
- Understand how to align experiences and skills to *Essential Demonstrated Behaviors*.
- Communicate your *essential* brand and *Essential Demonstrated Behaviors*.

Definition

Essential Demonstrated Behaviors: Past behaviors and experiences that show *how* you have handled specific tasks or challenges that will be telling of your performance in your next role or your potential in the field.

Identify Relevant Experiences and Skills

Identifying relevant experiences and skills is the first step to building an ability to articulate your experiences in relation to your *Essential Demonstrated Behaviors.*

You have gained relevant experiences and skills in other roles or through formal education that can be transferred to your next opportunity. Transferable skills and experiences are ones that show you have exhibited this skill or experience in a similar situation. These are important in order for you to align your experience with an organization's needs. Often these experiences and skills have an action verb included in the phrase. Refer back to the appendix for the list of action verbs discussed in chapter one.

A simple formula to identify your relevant experiences and skills is as follows:

- Make a list of action verbs you want to highlight based on your day in a specific role or experience you want in your resume or interview using action verbs. A few questions to consider to get you started include:
  - » What did you do?
  - » How did you do it?
  - » Who did you interact with?

- Determine if there are additional skills or experiences learned from this job.
- Determine action phrases in your list (see the next page for suggestions).

 CINDY'S EXAMPLE

We will use Cindy's first job to outline a process flow of a typical day, including specific actions using action verbs, to demonstrate how this might look for her. Next we can identify the *key* action phrases.

1. **Analyzed performance** to create daily report and **communicated information** via written reports and during weekly accountability meetings
2. **Reconciled daily accounts**
3. **Conducted quality check** on performance and transaction data
4. Based on an investment manager request, **developed a custom portfolio report including an in-depth review of financial data, trends**, and recommendations
5. **Collaborated with other departments** to share best ideas and leverage consistencies
6. **Calculated performance metrics** and **developed formulas** for the custom portfolio report

From this we learn that she gained the following experiences and skills: ability to perform analysis, accounting principles, creating and communicating reports, problem solving, and developing strategies.

ACTION PHRASE	RELEVANT EXPERIENCE / SKILL
<ul><li>Analyzed performance</li><li>In-depth review of financial data, trends, and recommendations</li></ul>	<ul><li>Ability to perform analysis</li></ul>
<ul><li>Reconciled daily accounts</li><li>Created daily report</li><li>Conducted quality checks</li><li>Communicated information via written reports and team meetings</li></ul>	<ul><li>Accounting principles</li><li>Creating performance reports</li><li>Communication</li></ul>
<ul><li>Created a custom portfolio report with results and recommendations</li></ul>	<ul><li>Ability to perform analysis</li><li>Development of strategies</li><li>Communication</li></ul>
<ul><li>Collaborated with other departments</li></ul>	<ul><li>Teamwork</li></ul>
<ul><li>Developed formulas for the custom portfolio report to address specific business questions</li></ul>	<ul><li>Problem solving</li><li>Technical knowledge (Microsoft Excel and accounting software)</li></ul>

If we apply the formula above and use the action verbs, we start to see a richer and clearer picture of the skills that have been acquired. If we sketch out a process flow of a typical day, including specific actions with action verbs, we can then identify the *key* action phrases and determine what additional experience could be highlighted.

 JOE'S EXAMPLE

Joe worked as a pool cleaning professional, and his initial description of his skills were as follows:

- Conducted daily hands-on pool cleaning and maintenance of pool and patio furniture
- Received calls from **customers in need** of monthly maintenance or problems that occurred with the pool cleaning system
- Worked to **solve the problem** with the customer to **find a solution** within their budget
- **Reviewed the outcome** with the owner
- Followed up with the customer to **ensure satisfaction**

From this we learn that he gained the following experiences and skills: customer service experience, problem solving, and experience cleaning and maintaining pools.

ACTION PHRASE	RELEVANT EXPERIENCE / SKILL
<ul><li>Interacting with customer</li><li>Customer satisfaction</li></ul>	<ul><li>Customer service experience</li></ul>
<ul><li>Solving problems</li><li>Analyzing outcomes</li></ul>	<ul><li>Problem solving</li></ul>
	<ul><li>Experience cleaning and maintaining pools</li></ul>

Let's look at another example.

 CHRIS' EXAMPLE

Chris worked as a cashier and sandwich maker at a local sandwich shop and he greeted and served guests, prepared food, and handled light paperwork.

If we sketch out a process flow of a typical day, we see the following *key* action phrases emerge:

- When guests arrived, I **greeted them cheerfully** and with a smile.
- **I explained any menu items** the customer had questions about and pointed out daily specials.
- I used the cash register to record the order, **computed the amount** of the bill, and then **collected payment** from guests.
- I prepared the sandwiches **according to instructions** and **specifications in a timely manner.**
- I followed up with the customer to **ensure satisfaction** and **resolved** any **customer concerns**.
- **I performed light paperwork duties** at the end of the day to close the register and **provided the manager with data collect to inform food ordering** based on the daily sales.
- **I trained new hires** on the sandwich-making processes and expectations.

ACTION PHRASE	RELEVANT EXPERIENCE / SKILL
<ul><li>Greeted them cheerfully</li><li>Followed up with the customer to ensure satisfaction</li><li>Resolved any customer concerns</li></ul>	<ul><li>Customer service experience</li></ul>

▪ Prepared the sandwiches according to instructions and specification in a timely manner	▪ Prepared items to clear specifications
▪ Collected data to inform food ordering based on the daily sales	▪ Experience with restaurant ordering systems
▪ Trained new hires	▪ Training and people development experience

From this we learn that he gained the following experiences and skills: customer service, training new hires, preparing items to clear specifications, and restaurant ordering systems.

Take a current or past job you have held and apply the exercise above to that job.

SKETCH OUT A PROCESS FLOW OF A TYPICAL DAY AND INCLUDE THE STEPS THAT OUTLINE THIS ACTION. THEN HIGHLIGHT THE *KEY* ACTION PHRASES.

1. _____

2. _____

3. _____

4. _____

5. _____

Next take the highlighted *key* action phrases and place them in the table below. Determine what experience or skill you can take away from those actions.

ACTION PHRASE	RELEVANT EXPERIENCE / SKILL

NOTE

If you're looking for a specific job or a specific industry, take a look at job postings to get a sense of what experiences they deem most important. Also make note of what language is being used to articulate the skill or experience.

eight

Unlocking Your Essential Demonstrated Behaviors

THE SECOND STEP TO ARTICULATING YOUR skills and experiences is aligning those experiences to *Essential Demonstrated Behaviors*. We've grouped them into the acronym PADLOCKS and together with your *Essential Branding Statement* (your *key*) they can unlock success.

Persuasion & Communication

Agility & Flexibility

Developing & Maintaining Relationships

Leadership & Accountability

Optimism & Resilience

Customer Focus

Knowledge Gathering & Analytical Thinking

Strategic Thinking

Essential Demonstrated Behaviors

DEMONSTRATED BEHAVIOR	WHAT IT MEANS
Persuasion & Communication	Ability to present, negotiate, teach, and/or communicate effectively with integrity
Agility & Flexibility	Ability to move, change, and adapt quickly and as needed while absorbing and integrating other points of view
Developing & Maintaining Relationships	Understand the dynamics of an organization, group, or team and balance your contribution as an individual as well as a member of a team Ability to establish relationships and leverage them to obtain a common goal
Leadership & Accountability	Ability to lead or guide a group to a certain task with or without actual overt managerial title Ability to make a decision and own outcomes of decision or action

Optimism & Resilience	Set an example of positive attitude Ability to overcome challenges and see opportunities where others may falter
Customer Focus	Identify whom your activity or job serves, what their needs are, and how you can best address those needs
Knowledge Gathering & Analytical Thinking	Gather and integrate the right kinds of information, think through different steps, and prioritize to derive actionable conclusions
Strategic Thinking	Build a bigger picture or approach to solve a problem or maximize an opportunity

Persuasion & Communication

Ability to present, negotiate, teach, and communicate effectively with integrity. Exceptional skills and behaviors often get lost when they can't be explained or clearly communicated with peers, managers, or organizations. It's not just about being good at what you do but also being able to explain what you do to others effectively, efficiently, or differently and in a way that pulls them in. This makes others want to take action and aligns them to a common goal.

EXAMPLE

While working at an internship in an accounting department, Sara makes some changes to streamline the system that records invoices.

☑ She also pulls together an organized, two-paragraph e-mail describing the changes made and sends it out to her manager and colleagues. Sara's manager forwards this on to a few of his colleagues, and she is then asked to come to a different department's team meeting and describe her updates. During the meeting she outlines the need for the change and how the benefits of the new system are relevant to them. At the end of the meeting, the two departments agree to continue to look to improve efficiencies.

☒ Since she doesn't tell anyone but her friends that she made the changes, people using the system are surprised and confused when they see the changes. In response to this issue, Sara sends an e-mail out to her team saying, "The system was really stupid, so I fixed it. Peace out, Sara." Other departments do not see the benefit to the changes and don't understand them. The process quickly falls apart, and people revert back to the previous system for conducting business.

Agility & Flexibility

Ability to move quickly, change, and adapt as needed, including the ability to absorb and integrate other points of view. Organizations are looking for employees who are willing to consider other people's point of view and incorporate a variety of perspectives when coming up with a plan or project. This sort of open-minded inclusiveness helps to generate new and more innovative ideas. Organizations are also looking for employees to be quick in their ability to change, learn new things, and respond to new and different situations.

 EXAMPLE

Debra takes a job at a causal retail clothing store known for its conservative but stylish clothes.

She has two friends that work in the same role in different stores and have told her, in detail, what the job is like. But when Debra sits down with her manager on the first day, the manager describes something completely different and says she's making some changes in this franchise to align more to current trends. In response Debra asks her more about why she's making the changes so she can better understand them. Then she describes to her manager where she sees clear differences in a way that shows she understands the differences and is excited to try the new approach and set an example. Debra even provides a few alternative suggestions based on her experience in another job.

This season the store manager has decided to feature combat boots with miniskirts (as seen in a fashion magazine). Debra does not ask for clarification to better understand the changes. She thinks this looks ridiculous and would never wear it or suggest it to customers. She refuses to promote this look in her area of the store and complains about how silly it looks to customers.

Developing & Maintaining Relationships

Understanding the dynamics of an organization, group, or team and balancing your contribution as an individual and as a member of a team. There are two key aspects of this behavior. First, you're willing to balance your own goals with the well-being of your team. There's a time and place for both individual objectives and a need to ensure you're considering what's best for your group, even if you work in a relatively independent role. No one wants to hire or work with someone who's only out for him or herself.

The second part of this behavior is a willingness to extend your professional community beyond what's immediately comfortable for both your own benefit and for the benefit of your team and the projects you're working on. Along with Persuasion and Communication, this behavior, when done well, requires you to negotiate and build relationships with people outside your in circle and to do so professionally.

 EXAMPLE

Allan has an internship at a large construction equipment firm focused on understanding process improvement and supply chain management.

During his first month, he sets up meetings all across the organization. They are short, introductory meetings where Allan spends twenty minutes asking others about why they chose this profession and their career paths and five minutes sharing his interests. In addition he looks for commonalities that he can use later to achieve goals and build a foundation to long-term relationships.

Allan spends 90 percent of his time catching up with his friends on the latest sports updates and upcoming fraternity events. When it comes time for Allan to work on a project that involves all the different departments in the company, he is not able to connect with his colleagues and his portion of the project fails.

Leadership & Accountability

Exhibiting the ability to lead or guide a group to a certain task with or without actual overt managerial title. This includes the ability to make and own a decision and the outcome of those decisions. Good organizations, big or small, work best when most of their members are willing to bear the responsibility of their individual and group performance. In contrast there's no one tougher to work with, manage, or work for than someone who refuses to take responsibility. You know this if you've ever worked on a school project as a part of a team where one team member doesn't pull his or her own weight and expects the rest to do it.

Leadership doesn't mean you need a job title that allows you to boss people around. It means even in situations where you have little official authority, you can to pave the way for others and lead (kindly and with respect for others, of course). Leaders have the social influence in which they can inspire and motivate others to accomplish a common task.

 EXAMPLE

Tamara is part of a university social group that volunteers to rehab abandoned houses in town once a month on Saturday mornings.

☑ Even when her friends are tired from a big Friday night out, she can rally them to action and run a car pool to the site. When the site manager suggests three things that could be done during the block of time they are there, she suggests a fourth the team could take on that would make a huge difference for the new homeowners. By encouraging the rest the group with both her actions and words, she motivates the team to exceed goals for the day.

☒ Tamara misses several trips to town to assist with rehabbing abandoned houses. On the months she does show up, she is an hour late. Rather than support her teammates, she instead complains a lot about the time it takes to complete the work. When she applies for internships, she talks about her experience with the program, but everyone who volunteered thinks of her as the no-show and would never ask her to be a part of a team or recommend her for a job.

Optimism & Resilience

Setting an example of a positive attitude and displaying an ability to overcome challenges by seeing opportunities where others may falter. No one can be happy about everything all the time. But consider those people who may have been on a team or extracurricular group with you who do nothing but complain. Negativity spreads throughout organizations rapidly and is pervasive. Whether justified or not, it becomes extraordinarily difficult to overcome and move past negativity. Employers are looking to hire people who they are confident will not add to this continuum but look for ways to move forward.

Resiliency is another aspect of this behavior. In the recent economy and social era, situations are changing faster than most of us can anticipate. It's virtually impossible to determine what change is next and how big or impactful it will be. Organizations look for people who are able to adapt to whatever change comes their way with grace and a good attitude. Again, we're not saying you can't be realistic and honest, but you can't be mired in a past expectation and not look forward to future opportunities.

 EXAMPLE

Alex's volleyball team had a great season, and the team has been practicing and preparing for their next game with their arch rival every night for a tournament match on Saturday. On Friday morning it's announced that the schedule has changed due to issues with the facilities, and they are now playing a different team.

☑ Alex comes to the Friday practice with some ideas on how to adapt to the new team's defensive style and outlines why this change is good for the team.

This is the third time this has happened and Alex is over all the drama. She doesn't show up to Friday practice, and she calls out sick from the Saturday game.

Customer Focus

Identifying whom your activity or job serves, what their needs are, and how you can best address those needs. Potential Essential, LLC is very passionate about the voice of the customer being heard and keeping the customer in mind to achieve effective and meaningful marketing. Any time you need to engage with someone else to meet your goals, you have a customer you need to showcase yourself to as an exceptional marketer. These interactions can be with a mentor, a teacher, or someone in your professional community. These may be brief or long encounters. All of these customers have needs and desires. Finding a way to align your goals with their needs leads to mutual success.

We are more successful and happier in life when we take the time to understand other's needs and seek to meet them. This behavior is the foundation for many other behaviors such as developing relationships, leadership, persuasion, and effective communication. The first step is to identify your key stakeholder or customer and then learn more about them. Once you learn about them, you can assess what you may have to offer them in order to build rapport and forge relationships. You may offer a referral to a restaurant, a solution to a problem, or even help with a favorite side project.

 EXAMPLE

After classwork Rosie makes money to pay for school by selling cable internet plans to small businesses over the phone. The group she works for has given her some basic training on how to interact during the calls. But Rosie realizes reading from a script most often leads to a hang up.

So instead she starts the conversation by asking the customer what's most frustrating about running their business. Then she asks what they find most satisfying. Most say they never have enough time to get everything done, and Rosie is able to offer service options that can make their business more efficient.

Being hung up on frequently is frustrating. So she tries to increase her sales by doubling the number of calls she makes in her free time, but Rosie continues to read the script each time she calls a business and misses the opportunities to increase her sales.

Knowledge Gathering & Analytical Thinking

Gathering and integrating the right kinds of information, thinking through different steps, and prioritizing information to derive actionable conclusions. This is the natural next step to customer focus. This behavior is also often referred to as critical thinking or problem solving. Again this is not just about what you do but the methodical way in which you think about solving a problem or maximizing an opportunity. Employers are looking for you to show that you can gather and organize objective facts and information, organize them, and then reach a solid conclusion.

 EXAMPLE

During the weekends Matt works the register at a pizza shop. The owner asked Matt if he could take some time to understand why business has been down this semester during quiet times at the register.

✓ When it's quiet Matt gets on the Internet and finds three competitors within a mile offering big coupons. He also finds some yelp.com reviews of the competitors saying they offered huge pieces of pizza compared to the shop he works at. You print out the coupons and the reviews, share them with the owner and suggest a competitive coupon might be needed.

He asks two of his friends, who tend to hang in the back and use the free Wi-Fi, what they think about the business. They say it looks fine to them. Matt has never liked their veggie pizza, so when his boss asks what information he found, Matt says he thinks people don't like the veggie pizza.

Strategic Thinking

Building a bigger picture approach to solving a problem or maximizing an opportunity. Not every job or opportunity will call for this behavior, especially at entry-level positions, but it's a remarkable behavior to build and exhibit for future growth. It is also the natural next step in the continuum of understanding your customer. This can be done by building facts and information in order to be analytical and fact based. It involves an understanding of customer needs, identifying opportunities to create competitive advantage, and then finally putting all the pieces together with your own approach to build a plan that will perform well. Think of it as trying to see how all the pieces of a puzzle might fit together before you actually do it and then making a plan to put the puzzle together in the shortest way.

EXAMPLE

Marian sings in a choir that's doing a large charity performance soon. Volunteers have convened in a church basement to put together thank-you bags for those that will attend and donate.

She notices that as people go around and fill the bags, everything is in the wrong order. The bags are at the end of the line instead of the beginning; none of the papers are folded and each person has to stop and fold a paper before they put it in the bag. It's taking twice as long as it could to get this project done. Marian asks everyone to take a five-minute break and reorganizes the supplies on the tables. Within an hour the job is done and the choir goes to brunch to celebrate.

She notices that as people go around and fill their bags, they're bumping into each other and wasting lots of time. It's annoying, but it's the way its set up and she just wants to get it done and go to practice.

Communicating Your *Essential* Brand, *Essential Demonstrated Behaviors*, and Experience

This process will help you articulate your value to prospective companies.

Communicating *Essential Demonstrated Behaviors*

Now that you have a general understanding of *key* behaviors that employers are seeking, how do communicate your *Essential Demonstrated Behaviors* to convey these *key* elements about *you*?

Start by using the *key* action phrases and relevant experiences you created earlier. Determine which *Essential Demonstrated Behaviors* you would align to your experiences in order to build an impactful example.

 CINDY'S EXAMPLE

When we look at Cindy's relevant experiences and skills, we can see several *Essential Demonstrated Behaviors* that each experience might be able to support.

ACTION PHRASE	RELEVANT EXPERIENCE/ SKILL	ESSENTIAL DEMONSTRATED BEHAVIORS
• Analyzed performance • In-depth review of asset analytics	• Perform analysis	• Knowledge Gathering & Analytical Thinking

• Reconciled daily accounts • Created daily report • Conducted quality checks • Communicated information via written reports and team meetings	• Account principles • Create performance reports • Communication	• Knowledge Gathering & Analytical Thinking • Persuasion & Communication
• Created a custom portfolio report with results/ recommendations	• Perform analysis • strategic • Communication	• Leadership & Accountability • Strategic Thinking • Customer Focus • Persuasion & Communication
• Collaborated with other departments	• Teamwork	• Developing & Maintaining Relationships
• Developed formulas for the custom portfolio report to address specific business questions	• Problem solving • Technical knowledge (Microsoft Excel and accounting software)	• Knowledge Gathering & Analytical Thinking

Below is how Joe's and Chris's *Essential Demonstrated Behaviors* might look based on their relevant experience and skills.

 JOE'S EXAMPLE

ACTION PHRASES	RELEVANT EXPERIENCE SKILL	ESSENTIAL DEMONSTRATED BEHAVIORS:
▪ Interacted with customer ▪ Customer satisfaction	▪ Customer service experience	▪ Customer Focus ▪ Persuasion & Communication
▪ Solved problems	▪ Problem solving	▪ Knowledge Gathering & Analytical Thinking

🔍 CHRIS'S EXAMPLE

ACTION PHRASES	RELEVANT EXPERIENCE / SKILL	ESSENTIAL DEMONSTRATED BEHAVIORS:
• Greeted them cheerfully • Followed up with the customer to ensure satisfaction • Resolved any customer concerns	• Customer service experience	• Customer Focus • Persuasion & Communication
• Prepared the sandwiches according to instructions and specification in a timely manner	• Prepared items to company specification and regulation requirements	• Leadership & Accountability

▪ Collected data to inform food ordering based on the daily sales	▪ Experience with restaurant ordering systems.	▪ Knowledge Gathering& Analytical Thinking
▪ Trained new hires	▪ Training and people development experience	▪ Persuasion & Communication ▪ Leadership & Accountability

Take the job you used to **create *key* action phrases** and determine which *Essential Demonstrated Behaviors* would apply.

ACTION PHRASES	RELEVANT EXPERIENCE / SKILL	ESSENTIAL DEMONSTRATED BEHAVIORS:

ACTION PHRASES	RELEVANT EXPERIENCE / SKILL	ESSENTIAL DEMONSTRATED BEHAVIORS:

nine

Pulling It All Together

IN ORDER TO INCREASE THE EFFECTIVENESS of your *essential* brand, it's important to consider when and where you should use each tool we have discussed. The objective is to provide a clear, concise, and consistent message about why you are the best choice for a role. We're taking the same approach big companies take. When companies consider the different ways (e.g. digital, print ads, or social media) to market a specific product, they must decide where to interact with the customer and with what message.

Essential Branding Statement + Essential Demonstrated Behaviors =
Success

Let's look at a popular consumer product like coffee. Starbucks, for example, has a website, Twitter account, Facebook page, in-store promotions, coffee sales in grocery stores, and branded items like coffee mugs and coffee machines. With each approach to interact with the customer, they provide a clear message of who they are and what they can offer (e.g. in-store experience, gift, grocery item, or driving through for a quick cup of coffee).

The same applies to your *Essential Branding Statement.* Below is a table that outlines where the *essential* branding sections and the *Essential Demonstrated Behaviors* are likely work best for you.

OPPORTUNITY	SECTION OF *ESSENTIAL BRANDING STATEMENT*	*ESSENTIAL* DEMONSTRATED BEHAVIORS
LinkedIn (or other online) profile	▪ *Essential Branding Statement* in background summary opening ▪ Strength statements in body of background	▪ Job experience summary ▪ Job experience list of responsibilities and achievements
Elevator pitch	▪ *Essential Branding Statement* ▪ *Motivational Force*	

Cover letters	• *Essential Branding Statement* in opening or closing sentence • Strength statement in body of letter aligned to their needs	• Opening or closing
Resume development	• *Essential Branding Statement* for objective statement • Strength statement in experience	• Job experience summary • Job experience list of responsibilities and achievements
In conversations with your Professional Community/Informational interviews	• *Motivational Force* to respond to why are you interested in this industry • *Guide* to respond to why are you interested in this company • Close the conversation with your *Essential Branding Statement*	• Addressing questions about your experience (see next section for more information)

| Formal interviews | ▪ *Motivational Force* to response to why are you interested in this industry
▪ *Guide* to respond to why are you interested in this company
▪ *Essential Branding Statement* | ▪ Addressing questions about your experience (see next section for more information) |
| Thank-you notes (example in next section) | ▪ *Essential Branding Statement*
▪ Strength statements | ▪ Emphasizing your experience and skills relevant to the opportunity (see next section for more information) |

CINDY'S EXAMPLE OF AN ELEVATOR PITCH AT CAREER FAIR

It's great to meet you! My name is Cindy Example, and I recently graduated from ABC College with a bachelor's of science degree in finance and accounting management. In my first job, I was able to deliver results by understanding my client's needs, and I'm excited about a career in which

I can use my skills to develop creative solutions that motivate others to save for the future.

 NOTE

It's important to align your *Essential Branding Statement* and *Essential Demonstrated Behavior* statements to a specific role. Determine the company's or hiring manager's needs and/or challenges so you can align your *Essential Branding Statement* and *Essential Demonstrated Behavior* to *their* needs, not just what *you* want.

CINDY'S COVER LETTER EXAMPLE

Cindy is applying to a financial company that is small, and she may want to discuss how her creative solutions and strategic ability can help attract more customers. If the company is very established and Cindy uncovers that one of their needs is to retain current clients, she would want to focus her ideas on how to motivate and encourage continued saving.

Below is an example cover letter Cindy might send to a large established company.

Cindy's Contact Information
Employer Contact Information **(if you have it)**

Dear Ms./Mr. Last Name:

I'm writing to inform you of my application for the position of manager of Financial Strategy posted on ABC.

In addition below are a few key strengths that I would bring to this position and your team: **(strength statements)**

- Ability to identify creative solutions based on customer needs to retain current clients
- Strategic thinker who can deliver short and long term goals
- Positive viewpoint that enables me to motivate others toward their goals and encourage continued saving

I use my ability to think strategically combined with my creativity to design financial planning solutions to allow people to enjoy life now and keep them motivated to save for the future. **(Branding Statement)** I'd love to find out more about the position you're looking to fill, and I would welcome the opportunity to further discuss how my skills can deliver results for XYZ Company. I can be reached at (555) 555-5555 or name@email.com.

Thanks for your consideration; I look forward to hearing from you soon!

Sincerely,

Cindy Example

ADDITIONAL EXAMPLE (CHRIS)

Chris' Contact Information
Employer Contact Information **(if you have it)**

Dear Ms./Mr. Last Name:

As a customer service expert in retail management, I bring the skills you need to fill the position for assistant manager position, requisition number 8764, which is posted on the XYZ website.

Requirements

- Strong interpersonal skills
- Bachelor's degree or two years of experience in retail
- Experience in customer service or retail sales associate

Qualifications

(Opportunity to include *Essential Demonstrated Behavior* with your experience)

- Ability to ensure customer satisfaction by addressing needs and resolving any customer concerns **(Customer Focus example)**
- Performed daily paper work and monthly analysis to assist with ordering **(Leadership and Accountability)**
- Accountable for training all new hires on technique and company policies **(Persuasion and Communication)**

It appears that there is a strong match between your requirements and my qualifications. I would like to meet you at your earliest convenience to discuss this opportunity. My resume is attached for your consideration.

Sincerely,

Chris Example

NOTE

We discuss how to align your *Essential Branding Statement* and *Essential Demonstrated Behaviors* in your cover letter, but we do not address structure or style elements. We have provided some references in the appendix for further information.

Communicating Your *Essential Branding Statement, Essential Demonstrated Behaviors*, and Experience

Resume Tips

As shown in the table above, your resume is a key place to carry through your *Essential Branding Statement*, strength statements, and *Essential Demonstrated Behaviors*.

 CINDY'S EXAMPLES OF EXPERIENCE ON HER RESUME

If we did not apply the *essential* branding to Cindy's resume, the bullets might look something like this:

- Reviewing performance and analysis
- Provide portfolio and asset analytics as requested by the investment managers

- Quality check valuation, performance, and transaction data
- Manual performance calculations when requested
- Create daily/monthly/quarterly reports
- Reconcile daily accounts as needed

The above articulates the actions performed by Cindy, but not how she achieved them, what the result of the action was, or what strengths she possesses. However, by using her *Essential Branding Statement* and *Essential Demonstrated Behaviors*, her resume can be much stronger and establish her brand with the hiring manager. Below is an example of the bullets that might be included.

- Utilized account principles and ability to perform analysis to provide daily reports, quality checks, and reconciling accounts
- Provided senior account managers with customized portfolio reports including analysis, conclusions, and recommendations
- Collaborated with other departs and led a monthly best practice sharing session to increase productive and reduce redundancies

ADDITIONAL EXAMPLE

Based on Joe's experience, his resume might include the following:

- Responded to customers' pool maintenance problems and used problem solving skills to provide customer focused solutions
- Provided routine pool cleaning and maintenance with superior service and increased return business

> ### NOTE
>
> In this book we discuss how to align your *Essential Branding Statement* and *Essential Demonstrated Behaviors* in your resume, but we do not address structure or additional *key* elements. We have provided some references in the appendix for further information.

Communicating *Essential Demonstrated Behaviors* at an Interview

As we discussed earlier, employers are looking to see if you can demonstrate a few of the *key* behaviors they feel the role requires and the company values. After the last section, you are practically there with your strong resume statements, online profile, and specific cover letters.

This section will help you organize strong examples that support your *essential* brand and show your *Essential Demonstrated Behaviors*. We recommend using the SAR format to communicate your *Essential Demonstrated Behaviors*. The SAR format is a clear and concise way to articulate your *essential* brand and *Essential Demonstrated Behaviors*.

Have around five SARs that you are able to recite in any situation and can use to address specific questions.

A SAR is a format and stands for:

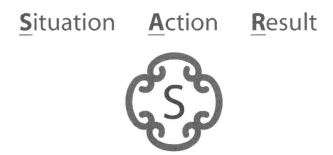

Situation: This is your opportunity to describe the circumstances and/or outline a challenge you had. This not the place to spend the majority of your time and provide too much detail. You will lose those who are listening and you will not be able provide the action and result. This can also be referred to as a challenge or a task at hand.

Action: Here is where you should articulate not only *what* you did but *how* you did it. Does this piece sound familiar? It's the *Essential Demonstrated Behaviors*. Spend the majority of your time here.

Result: It's imperative not to forget this piece. This shows the value of your action. You may have a tangible result (e.g., increase sales, develop efficiencies, improved a process, more customers) or a key lesson you obtained that show the importance of your involvement.

CINDY'S EXAMPLE

Take the bullets from Cindy's resume:

- Utilized account principles and ability to perform analysis to provide daily reports, quality checks, and reconciling accounts
- Provided senior account managers with customized portfolio reports including analysis, conclusions, and recommendations
- Collaborated with other departs and led a monthly best practice sharing session to increase productivity and reduce redundancies

We can expand on these bullets to create a SAR to address interview questions.

SITUATION	ACTION (ESSENTIAL DEMONSTRATED BEHAVIOR)	RESULT
In order to ensure quality and high performance, management required daily and monthly reports of the portfolio assets retained by the company.	I utilized accounting principles and analysis to provide daily/monthly reports, quality checks, and reconciling accounts.	This resulted in clear communication at all levels on the performance of accounts, allowing adjustments to be made that increased profitability.
Senior account managers' need to understand multiple investment options for key clients.	I provided senior account managers with customized portfolio reports including analysis, conclusions, and recommendations.	This allowed the account managers to provide their customers with innovative solutions to meet their investor's needs. This set them apart from our competition and increased investments with our company.
Several departments were conducting similar work and didn't share the key learnings between departments.	I collaborated with other departments and led a monthly best practice sharing session.	This led to increased productivity and trust among departments and reduced redundancies

95

Take a situation you want to share and use
this format to develop your SARs.

SITUATION	ACTION (*ESSENTIAL DEMONSTRATED BEHAVIOR*)	RESULT

ten

The Interview

THE PROCESS OF INTERVIEWING HAS TWO parts. First your role is to convey your *potential* and why you would be *essential* to the organization. The interviewer's goal is to evaluate you on multiple aspects, including skills, future potential, experience, and organizational fit.

First Impressions

 In any interaction with a prospective employer or someone to build your professional community, remember that first impressions count! This includes not just in-person interactions but also in e-mail, phone conversations, and other interactions you may meet in the company. If we think about a consumer brand, when you interact with them via e-mail, customer service, website, in the store, or someone you meet who works there, you are getting an impression of what this company is and determining if you want to purchase anything from him or her. This is the same for a company when they are looking to hire someone.

As we discussed in the *essential* branding section, when a brand resonates with the customer, it starts the process of being the "product of choice." We want you to become the "candidate of choice" for your next opportunity.

As you start to communicate your *essential* brand with prospective employers, keep the following in mind:

- Any time you interact (in person, by mail, phone, or e-mail) with a prospective employer, remember they are evaluating you and your *essential* brand!
- Be respectful in the way you dress and the way you conduct yourself.
- Be positive, upbeat, and professional.

 NOTE

If you feel comfortable wearing what you are wearing to the interview out with your friends for drinks at a club at the end of the day, this is *not* professional attire. If you feel like you need to run home and change in order to go to a club with your friends, this *is* professional attire. Consider that most likely someone your age is not interviewing you. Part of assessing your *potential* and judging your *essential* brand will include what you wear to the interview.

See what others see. What is your *essential* brand with your online presence?

- Clean up your online profile! The first thing a recruiter or HR person will do is google you (yes, they know how to use social media too). Don't get caught with photos that you would not want to show at a prospective job interview. Prospective employers may also check your profiles after the interview; don't think that once you have the interview, you're safe to go wild on social media.
- A few common reasons for rejecting applicants include postings with poor grammar and/or spelling, lack of written communication skills, inappropriate photos (e.g. public intoxication, over the top displays of affection), information suggesting drug use or alcohol abuse, lying about qualifications, unprofessional screen names, and racist, sexist or offensive comments.

 EXAMPLE

A new graduate in the teaching profession was very excited to get called back for a second interview and felt that it went very well after having received positive signals. However, a week later she was notified she would not be getting the position. Upon request for feedback, they said her online profile did not meet with their vision of their educators. Between interviews she had posted a photo of her and her friends with beer at a bar at the beach.

While we agree your personal life *should* be personal, when you post information about yourself and others, it's no longer private and may not be consistent with the *essential* brand you want to convey as a professional.

Tips on Interviewing

- Research: Do your research on the company, role, and interviewer (if possible). There are many ways to research companies and employers.
  - » Periodicals and web articles provide timely information about the company or the industry
  - » Company website
  - » Current employees
  - » LinkedIn or Facebook Page
  - » News articles on Google
  - » Annual reports
  - » Financial analyst reports
  - » Chamber of Commerce (if it's a small local company)
  - » Online databases and library resource (see appendix for more information)

- Practice: Like any other activity, you need to practice and get feedback from another person. You might be surprised that you have habits interviewers find distracting. For example you may say "um" frequently, laugh nervously, state your point over and over, or fidget with your pen. Ways to practice include the following:
  - » Have a friend or family member ask you typical interview questions.
  - » Practice saying your SARs out loud.
  - » Video a mock interview.

NOTE

Consider what types of *Essential Demonstrated Behaviors* align with the opportunity and company values. Ensure that your SARs can address them, or have a plan on how you would quickly gain that experience.

Refrain from reciting memorized answers. Instead have key bullets for your SARs. If your answers are too robotic, you will sound stiff and nervous as opposed to conversational and confident. A skilled interviewee can align their answers to behavioral questions during the interview to more effectively meet the opportunity.

Plan ahead so you are on time.

- Get clear directions.
- Know where to park and who to see when you arrive.
- Plan to arrive ten to fifteen minutes early.

Connect.

- Be polite to the receptionist and/or recruiter. You might be surprised how many people have not been hired because they were rude or talked down to the receptionist. The receptionist or recruiter can also be a crucial source of information for the next round of interviews!
- Greet the interviewer cordially.
- Connect with the interviewer up front. Ask about them!
- Expect small talk to break the ice. Most interviewers will attempt to put you at ease by asking you questions in the beginning about you or your resume (which will be

addressed shortly). Be prepared to discuss a few current events. Don't forget this is still part of the interview, so don't share unprofessional activities in your weekend.

- Be professional in your interactions and show your personality.

EXAMPLE

Balance professional with your personality. A good example of going to the "professional extreme" is when Dawn was interviewing for one of her first marketing jobs. She had done all the analysis, prep work, and research on the brand and the people part of the brand. Dawn practiced her answers and was confident in her delivery of them. However, she didn't get the job because during the interview she was so professional she never gave them any indication of who she was. The brand that she was trying to build failed, in part, because she had not added in her *Motivational Force* and only discussed her skills and experience in very clinical terms. Dawn didn't show the "how" behind her experiences or what she was about.

Maintain proper body language.

- Sit up straight and maintain good, confident posture.
- Avoid fidgeting or nervous habits that can be distracting (snapping a pen cap, bouncing your knee up and down, chewing gum, playing with your hair, etc.).
- Smile and laugh when appropriate, but watch out for nervous laughter.

- Maintain eye contact.
- Avoid monotone and retain a confident and positive tone.
- Show your interest in the role by emphasizing key words or phrases that demonstrate your passion.

Types of Interview Questions

There are several kinds of questions that can be asked during an interview (open-ended, closed-ended [yes/no], comprehension questions, and alternate choice). The three most common types of questions are opening questions, behavior-based questions, and theoretical interview questions. Most companies use a mix of these three types with a heavier emphasis on behavior-based questions. Opening questions and behavioral-based questions provide an outstanding opportunity for you to relay your *essential* brand and *Essential Demonstrated Behaviors*.

Definitions

Opening questions: open-ended questions used typically in the beginning of the interview to set the stage and to put the interviewee at ease.

Behavior-based questions: designed to predict future performance based on performance in a similar situation. They are mostly related to "how" activities occurred.

Theoretical (situational) questions: place the interviewee in a hypothetical situation. These questions are more likely to determine what a candidate says they will do (i.e., job activities) vs how they have handled similar situations.

Let's take a look at a few examples of each type of question and how you can apply your *essential* brand and *Essential Demonstrated Behaviors*.

Opening Questions

Two common opening questions are, "tell me about yourself" and "please review your resume." Don't be fooled into a false sense of security; these questions are important to the interview, and if you are not concise with your answers, you will use up time that could be spent on other important elements. In addition, how you respond to this question sets the tone for the rest of the interview.

The "tell me about yourself" question is the time for you to provide the interviewer with *key* elements from your *Essential Branding Statement* and show them a bit of your personality.

This is *not* the time for you to go into where you were born and how you love cats! Adding in *some* personal of information is welcome so the interviewer can get an idea of who you are, but this is *your* chance to present your *essential* brand in the interview process and convey why you are the "candidate of choice."

With the "please review your resume" question, you should be able to review your *key* strengths and *Essential Demonstrated Behaviors* related to the specific role in three to five minutes. Don't waste precious time reviewing a resume in-depth, and assume that the interviewer has read it prior to the interview. Many interviewers ask the question just as a warm up. However, it is your opportunity to share with him or her the skills and experiences you have gained through the jobs listed on your resume.

 EXAMPLE

During my summer internship at the XYZ ad agency, I learned communication skills and really honed in on my ability to work at all levels of the organization (supports "worked at XYZ ad agency as the assistant to the copywriter").

Behavior-based Questions

When asked behavior-based questions, this is a great opportunity for you to use your SARs and provide examples of your *Essential Demonstrated Behaviors.*

Below are several common behavior-based questions from interviews and how they align with *Essential Demonstrated Behaviors.*

ESSENTIAL DEMONSTRATED BEHAVIOR	WHAT IT MEANS	EXAMPLE INTERVIEW QUESTIONS
Persuasion & Communication	Ability to present, negotiate, teach, and communicate effectively and with integrity	▪ Give an example of a time where you needed to use your verbal communication skills to get your point across.

ESSENTIAL DEMONSTRATED BEHAVIOR	WHAT IT MEANS	EXAMPLE INTERVIEW QUESTIONS
		<ul><li>Tell how you communicated with someone who clearly didn't like you.</li><li>Give an example of your negotiation skills.</li><li>Give an example of your approach to communication across a team and to your management.</li><li>Give an example of a system you've used to communicate with peers or managers. How have you improved upon it?</li><li>Describe a time when you failed to meet a deadline and how you handled that.</li></ul>
Agility & Flexibility	Ability to move quickly, change, and adapt as needed and absorb and integrate other points of view	<ul><li>Give an example of a time where you had to conform to a policy or idea you didn't agree with.</li><li>Give an example of a time where you had to change your actions in response to a change in your environment.</li></ul>

ESSENTIAL DEMONSTRATED BEHAVIOR	WHAT IT MEANS	EXAMPLE INTERVIEW QUESTIONS
		<ul><li>Give an example of an innovation solution to a problem and how you achieved it.</li><li>Give an example of a time where you had to implement a change.</li><li>Tell about a time your supervisor was not satisfied with your work. What actions did you take?</li><li>Give an example when your activities were interrupted by unforeseen events. How did you handle that?</li></ul>
Developing & Maintaining Relationships	Understanding the dynamics of an organization, group, or team and balancing your contribution as an individual as well as being a member of a team	<ul><li>What did you do in your last job to be more effective with organization and planning?</li><li>What have you done in the past to contribute to a teamwork environment?</li><li>Do you like to work on group or solo projects?</li></ul>

ESSENTIAL DEMONSTRATED BEHAVIOR	WHAT IT MEANS	EXAMPLE INTERVIEW QUESTIONS
		<ul><li>When you're new to an organization, how do you go about becoming part of things?</li><li>Give an example in which you positively influenced others in a direction you needed them to go.</li><li>What place or part do you usually take on a team?</li><li>Give an example of a time where you had to turn around the trajectory of a team with a negative attitude.</li><li>Describe a time where you needed to pull resources together not under your direct control.</li><li>Describe a time where you had to resolve a conflict.</li><li>Describe a time where you've had to build rapport.</li><li>Give an example of an accomplishment you're most proud of and why.</li></ul>

ESSENTIAL DEMONSTRATED BEHAVIOR	WHAT IT MEANS	EXAMPLE INTERVIEW QUESTIONS
		<ul><li>Give an example of when you've had to teach someone a new skill and how you went about it.</li><li>Give an example of a time when someone on your team wasn't pulling their weight and how you handled it.</li></ul>

ESSENTIAL DEMONSTRATED BEHAVIOR	WHAT IT MEANS	EXAMPLE INTERVIEW QUESTIONS
Leadership & Accountability	Exhibiting the ability to lead or guide a group to a certain task with or without actual overt managerial authority	<ul><li>Give a time where you had to speak up and how you handled it.</li><li>Give an example of a time where you had to go above and beyond to achieve a goal.</li><li>Give an example of a time where you had to bend or break rules and why.</li><li>Give an example of a time where you had to set a goal and achieve it.</li><li>Give an example of one of the most important decisions of your life and how you made the decision.</li><li>Give an example of a time where you had to take initiative or be innovative.</li><li>Give an example of an accomplishment you're most proud of and why.</li></ul>

ESSENTIAL DEMONSTRATED BEHAVIOR	WHAT IT MEANS	EXAMPLE INTERVIEW QUESTIONS
Optimism & Resilience	Setting an example of positive attitude and displaying an ability to overcome challenges and see opportunities where others may falter	<ul><li>Give an example of a time where you had to motivate others.</li><li>Give an example of a time when others you worked with (like your team) were negative and how you turned that around.</li><li>Describe a situation where you faced a significant challenge and how you overcame it.</li><li>Describe a time where someone senior to you did not buy into an important idea and how you worked to change his or her viewpoint.</li><li>Tell how you work under pressure.</li><li>Describe a stressful situation and how you coped.</li><li>What's your attitude about life? Work?</li><li>What ways have you found to go about making your work more energizing and enjoyable?</li><li>Give an example of how you minimize stress.</li></ul>

ESSENTIAL DEMONSTRATED BEHAVIOR	WHAT IT MEANS	EXAMPLE INTERVIEW QUESTIONS
Customer Focus	Identifying whom your activity or job serves, what the needs are, and how you can best address those needs	▪ Give an example of how you had to read a customer and guide your actions by understanding his or her needs. ▪ Give an example of a time where you had to bend or break rules and why. ▪ Talk about a time where a customer was unhappy; how did you deal with the situation? ▪ How did you identify and understand a customer? ▪ Give an example of the most creative way you've gone about solving a customer's problem.

ESSENTIAL DEMONSTRATED BEHAVIOR	WHAT IT MEANS	EXAMPLE INTERVIEW QUESTIONS
Knowledge Gathering & Analytical Thinking	Gathering and integrating the right kinds of information; thinking through different steps and prioritizing objective information to derive actionable conclusions	▪ Tell about a time you couldn't finish a task because you didn't have enough information and the steps you took. ▪ Give an example of a time where you had to be very vigilant and aware in an environment and respond.
		▪ Give an example of a time where you needed to use fact-finding skills to reach success. ▪ Tell about a time where you had to carefully analyze a situation to guide actions. ▪ Give an example of a problem and how you solved it. ▪ Give an example of one of the most important decisions of your life and how you made the decision.

ESSENTIAL DEMONSTRATED BEHAVIOR	WHAT IT MEANS	EXAMPLE INTERVIEW QUESTIONS
Strategic Thinking	Building a bigger picture plan or approach to solving a problem or maximizing an opportunity	<ul><li>Give an example of a time where you used good logic or judgment in solving a problem.</li><li>Give an example of one of the most important decisions of your life and how you made the decision.</li><li>Give an example of a time where you had to be relatively quick with a decision.</li></ul>
		<ul><li>Give an example of a project where you had to establish priorities.</li><li>Give an example of a time where one of your suggestions was put into practice. How did you get there?</li><li>Give an example of how you've handled a variety of assignments and describe the results.</li></ul>

Theoretical (Situational) Questions

These questions are more likely to determine what a candidate says they will do (i.e., job activities) vs how they have handled similar situations. In some cases, there may even be a case study for you to review and present your analysis and recommendations.

Theoretical (Situational) Questions

1. Here's the situation. What would you do?
2. If you were in this situation, what would you do?
3. If you are given the following information, how would you solve the problem?

Here is an opportunity for you to work in *key* elements from your *Essential Branding Statement* and use *Essential Demonstrated Behaviors* to support how you would address these situations.

Out-of-bounds Questions

So you have prepared and prepared for the typical interview questions. What do you do if a prospective employer intentionally or inadvertently tosses an out-of-bounds question your way?

As defined by Title VII of the Civil Rights Act of 196, it is illegal (and inappropriate) for employers to consider an applicant's race, color, religion, sex, age, or national origin when making an employment decision. Therefore employers should not ask you questions about any of those topics. However, it is acceptable to volunteer information interviewers would otherwise be illegal to ask.

It happens! Think about how you want to address them so you aren't thrown off your game.

When responding to such questions, assess the situation and do your best to determine the reason for the question. Sometimes you may decide that you are comfortable answering the question. Other times you may want to try to deflect the inquiry.

Here are three strategies to consider.

1. Avoid answering the question and instead respond to the possible intent behind the question. When doing so it's best to tactfully rephrase the question into a legal one before answering. Try to figure out what the interviewer *really* wants to know. For example, if the interviewer asks if you are married (which is an illegal question), a clever way to answer would be, "If you mean to ask if I will be committed to my career and be available when needed to support the team, then yes."

2. Since the question is an illegal one, you can always be direct and refuse to answer, indicating that you are within your rights to do so. Be careful not to come off as hostile, especially if it seemed like an honest mistake.

3. Answer the question and move on, but only answer the question if you truly are comfortable providing the information.

Definition

Out of Bounds Question: [10] Employers should not ask any of the following because choosing not to hire a candidate based on any of these is discrimination.

- Race
- Color
- Sex
- Religion
- National origin
- Birthplace
- Age
- Disability
- Marital/family status
- Sexual orientation (in most states)

Interviewing Has Two Parts

You should always have several well-thought-out questions prepared ahead of time. If you don't ask questions during the interview process, the interviewer(s) may wonder if you understand the role and if you are serious about the position and company. This is also your opportunity to demonstrate the research you have done on the company. A few categories and example questions to consider are as follows:

General company

- What do you see ahead for your company in the next five years?
- How do you see the future for this industry?

- What do you consider are your firm's most important assets?
- What can you tell me about your new product or plans for growth?

Questions about the interviewer (everyone likes to talk about their personal career journey)

- Why did you choose this company?
- What was your career path?
- What is the most motivating aspect of this industry?

Role clarity

- How does X currently get performed in your company?
- I notice on your website or annual report that you are moving toward X; how does this role impact that?
- What happened to the last person who held this job?
- What is the overall structure of the company and how does your department fit the structure?
- What are the career paths in this department?
- Could you describe a typical day or week in this position? Who is the typical client or customer I would be dealing with?
- What does success look like at the end of twelve months in this role?

Competitor questions

- How do you rate your competition?
- What are strengths and weaknesses of your competition?

Align your *essential* brand to company needs questions

- What types of skills do you *not* already have onboard that you're looking to fill with a new hire?
- How can this role assist with business challenges in the organization?
- What have been the department's successes in the last couple of years?
- What would you consider are most important aspects of this job?
- What are the skills and attributes you value most for someone being hired for this position?
- Where have successful employees previously in this position progressed to within the company?
- What are the most immediate challenges of the position that need to be addressed in the first three months?

Next Step Questions

- What are the next steps in the interview process?
- May I have your contact information?

 NOTE

It's very important to get their business card (or contact information) at the end of the interview. Otherwise it can difficult to follow up.

NOTE

The questions and techniques for addressing them do not change if the interview is via the phone or virtual. A few things to keep in mind if it's a phone interview include the following:

- Do not smoke, chew gum, or eat.
- Have water handy in case you need it.
- Find a quiet place where you will not be disturbed.
- Dress professionally even if it's a phone call to set the tone in your mind.
- Stand, if possible, to increase your energy.
- Keep responses concise and clear.
- Since it's harder to pick up on responses (both yours and theirs), ask questions to clarify or if you need more information.
- Have the same resources available that you would have during an in-person interview (e.g. resume, pad of paper and pen, questions you want to ask).

Final Steps in the Interview Process

Once the interview is over, you still have some work to do and opportunities to solidify your *essential* brand.

Send a thank-you note immediately after the interview. If you miss the twenty-four hour window, send an e-mail right away. Late is better than no thank-you note. There is some debate whether snail mail or e-mail is the preferred medium. There are two schools of thought on handwritten notes:

- Makes you stand out from the crowd and can be seen as more intimate
- Can possibly make you look like you are out of touch and potentially not as savvy as your competition

The important part is that you send a thank-you note. You can gauge the culture of the company during the interview to determine what media is right for that interview.

 NOTE

If you choose to send a snail mail note, be sure you have the accurate address before you leave to ensure it doesn't get lost in the mailroom. In large corporations mail could get lost or overlooked.

In the thank-you letter, be sure you also include why you are a good fit for the job and company. Customize you *Essential Branding Statements* and *Essential Demonstrated Behaviors* to the position and company to make sure you are addressing the interviewers' needs and concerns. This will show you were listening during the interview and also strengthen your message. If you missed an opportunity to stress an experience or skill that you feel is important to the role, you can also include this information in the note.

Always make sure you proofread your note to ensure you have the tone you want and that you haven't missed any grammar or spelling errors. Even better, get a friend or family member with these skills to proofread your note.

CINDY'S EXAMPLE THANK-YOU NOTE WITH *ESSENTIAL BRANDING STATEMENT* ELEMENTS

Cindy's Contact Information
Employer Contact Information

Dear Mr./Ms. Last Name:

I wanted to thank you for the time you spent with me regarding the assistant financial planner position with XYZ Company. The role, as you presented it, seems to be a very good match for my skills and interests. In addition to my enthusiasm, I will bring to the position the following: (**strength statements**)

- Ability to identify creative solutions based on customer need
- Strategic thinker who can deliver short and long term goals
- Positive viewpoint that enables me to motive others toward their goals

I use my ability to think strategically combined with my creativity to design financial planning solutions to allow people to enjoy life now, and keeping them motivated to save for the future. (***Essential Branding Statement***)

The innovative approach to financial management that you described confirmed my desire to work with XYZ Company! (**aligned to her *Motivational Force***) I am very interested in working for you and look forward to hearing from you about this position.

Sincerely,

Cindy Example

Additional Follow-Up After Interview

During the interview hopefully you requested next steps and the interviewer provided you with a timeline. If they stated they would contact you in seven days, it's perfectly acceptable to remind them of the timing and reiterate your interest in the job. Some companies and hiring managers gauge how interested candidates are in the role and company by waiting to see who checks in. Don't be pushy or aggressive. Instead be clear and succinct in a quick e-mail or phone call.

 EXAMPLE

Mr./Ms. Last Name,

I hope you're having a great week.

You mentioned that you would be finalizing a hiring decision on the sale representative position this week. I'm still very excited about the position and wanted to check in with you regarding the next steps in the interview process.

And certainly if I may provide any additional information to support your decision-making process, please let me know!

Sincerely,

Your Name

Second Interviews

Importance of a Second Interview

The second is the next step and sometimes the final step in obtaining a job offer. However, it's not uncommon for there to be a third of fourth interview for a very competitive position.

Be prepared that you may or may not receive an offer during this interview. This varies widely by company and industry norms.

Employer Goals for Second Interviews

They will potentially look for a few things such as your unique qualities compared with other candidates, enthusiasm and passion, specific skills for the role, organization, and team fit. They may discuss salary, vacation, other benefits, employment guidelines (e.g. drug test, personality test requirements), and reimbursement of any travel expense. This is your opportunity to ask clarifying questions but not the time to negotiate on these items. This should wait until the offer is given.

The interview may consist of individual interviews (e.g. senior leadership or human resource manager) or panel discussions with other managers or potential colleagues. Additionally a case study review or other task may be conducted to further assess your skills. If these companies have manufacturing or operations onsite, you may be given a tour of the facilities. It is also not uncommon for a social setting to be part of the process including lunch or dinner, so be sure you are comfortable in those situations.

NOTE

Now is the time to use your very best interpersonal communication skills! In this step make sure you let them see your personality and what you are passionate about. Since they are looking for "fit" as much as they are evaluating you in comparison to other candidates, it's important that they understand who you are and how you can be of value to their organization. Be a little more relaxed in this stage, but remember this is *still* an interview and you will need to professionally convey your *essential* brand and *Essential Demonstrated Behaviors*.

Definition

Organizational and cultural team fit: both refer to the process of determining if you will be a good fit for the team and the company's culture.

Your Goals for Second Interviews

This is your chance to make sure you want to work with the organization, will have access to advancement opportunities, and view its culture firsthand by meeting others in the company and asking thoughtful questions. In addition you should continue to deliver your *Essential Branding Statements* during your interactions and follow up on any items that you did not have the opportunity to convey in the first interview.

Preparing for Second Interviews

If possible, obtain the agenda, structure of the day, and individuals involved in the interview process in advance. It's helpful for preparation, but be ready for last minute changes due to people's schedule and other urgent matters. Do additional research on the company, senior leadership, and the individuals who will be involved in the interview. (See resource section of the appendix.)

In addition, review your notes and original job posting from the first interview. If there were any questions you had a difficult time addressing, make sure that you have solidified your responses. Also make sure to stress any *key* skills or experience that the interviewer stated as important to the position during the first interview.

It is OK to use the same SARs that you used in the first interview and expand on them as opposed to feeling like you need a new example each time. Also add a few additional SARs based on your new knowledge of the company and position to customize your *essential* brand and further emphasize why you are the "candidate of choice."

 NOTE

In this book we don't discuss the offer or negotiating the offer but have provided some references in the appendix of the book.

eleven

Understanding & Evaluating Opportunities

WE ALL KNOW WE NEED A job, but it's important to reframe it in a way that allows us to determine what the job has to offer you so that you can evaluate your various opportunities and understand what a best fit is for the short and long term.

It's OK if your first job isn't your ideal job if it's a step in the right direction of where you might want to go. You can evaluate the opportunity in various ways using the tools we covered to establish your *essential* brand. Ensure the opportunity will build on your *essential* brand and the direction you want to go.

Here are a few ways to evaluate your opportunities:

- From the perspective of skill set, what types of different skills are you increasing or filling a gap in your education?
- Area of interest: does the role allow you greater access to your areas of interest? For instance if your goal is to work with cancer patients and you're doing hospital administration, is there a capacity to work more closely with cancer patients?

- Money: it pays your bills while you figure out how to get closer to your goal! Something to keep in mind here is if you forget that the role itself wasn't helping you reach your goal, you risk forgetting to develop a timely exit plan or next-steps plan.

Look for alternatives to continue your momentum and gain experience like volunteering, attending community classes, and networking. Be aware you're going to have to spend time and energy above and beyond your day job to keep going toward your goals.

Evaluating the Opportunity

Core Values: Do the company's values align with your core values?

- This can sometimes be found on the organization's website.
- Ask the HR person or recruiter to provide you with characteristics of the company as if the company were a person.

Key Strengths

- Are your strengths compatible with the role? (For example, you aren't a detail person and this is a data entry role.)
- Does the job description wording match any of the key words or phrases you have received from an assessment of your strengths?
- When you tell a friend or family about the option, do you feel yourself get excited?
- Do others tell you that you light up when you mention the opportunity?

Motivational Force

- Does the opportunity or company align with your *Motivational Force*?
  - » This can sometimes be found on their website or their annual report.
  - » Ask the HR person or recruiter for the company vision.
- Do you have to sell yourself and others on the opportunity? If so, it might be because it doesn't align with your *Motivational Force*.

Guide

- Does the opportunity align with your *Guide*?
- Would you do this role if you won the lottery? If so it aligns with your *Guide*.
- Does the opportunity get you closer to your goals?
- Do you acquire new skills or experiences?
- Do you increase your professional community within a particular focus?

Questions to ask yourself about different companies

- What size (small, mid, large, private, public, nonprofit, shareholders, etc.)?
- How much accountability?
- How much energy will it take? Will you need to reserve some energy to get to the next step, or will you give it all now as it's headed in the direction you want to go?
- What are the opportunities for advancement?
- What is the salary range and associated benefit package?

Here is a simple way to evaluate opportunities and ensure they are moving you in the direction you want to go:

Potential and *Essential* Opportunity Evaluation Grid

OPPORTUNITY	OFFERS NEW SKILLS OR EXPERIENCE	SIZE OF COMPANY	STRUCTURE OF COMPANY	OTHER FACTORS (E.G., IMMEDI-ATE FINANCIAL NEED, TRAVEL REQUIREMENTS)			

OPPORTUNITY	IN-LINE MOTIVATIONAL FORCE	IN-LINE WITH *GUIDE*	USE STRENGTHS	POSITIVE IN-FLUENCE ON ESSENTIAL BRAND			

twelve

Wrapping It Up and Keeping the Momentum

ALL THE STEPS WE WILL SHARE with you add up to three pretty simple equations:

(Unique ID + Motivational Force + *Guide*) X Communication =
***Essential* Branding Statement**

(Action Phrases + Relevant Experiences and Skills) X Behaviors =
Essential Demonstrated Behaviors

Essential Branding Statement + *Essential Demonstrated Behaviors* =
Success

You have discovered your core values and strengths. You've learned how to create your *essential* brand and the ability to use *Essential Demonstrated Behaviors* to land your next job. You are well on your way on your career journey!

We strongly encourage you to continue to evolve your *essential* brand as you gain more skills and experience. Once you are in the workforce, you will need to enhance and develop your skills and experience. You will use it moving forward to solidify your position in the organization, get recognized for your work, and obtain the next role. We talk more about this at www.potentialessential.com and it will be the focus of the next book.

Discover your *potential* and become *essential* in your new role. Good luck!

Appendix

Resume Resources

- *Unbeatable Resumes: America's Top Recruiter Reveals What Really Gets You Hired* by Tony Beshara
- Career websites: www.jobsearch.about.com, www.monster.com, www.indeed.com, www.careerbuilder.com
- *Resume Magic, 4th Ed: Trade Secrets of a Professional Resume Writer* by Susan Britton Whitcomb

Interview Resources

- *201 Best Questions to Ask on Your Interview* by John Kador
- *101 Great Answers To The Toughest Interview Questions* by Ron Fry
- *Interview for Success* by Caryl Krannich
- Career websites: www.jobsearch.about.com, www.monster.com, www.indeed.com, www.careerbuilder.com

Networking Resources

- *Social Networking for Career Success: Using Online Tools To Create a Personal Brand* by Miriam Salpeter
- Career websites: www.jobsearch.about.com, www.monster.com, www.indeed.com, www.careerbuilder.com
- *How To Write a Killer LinkedIn Profile and 18 Mistakes To Avoid* by Brenda Bernstein
- *Career Distinction—Stand out by Building your Brand* by William Arruda and Kristen Dixson
- *24 Networking Tips That Actually Work* by James Clear www.passivepanda.com/networking-tips

Online databases or library resources

- ABI Inform Complete
- Academic OneFile
- Academic Search Premier
- Alacra Store
- Company Insight Center (CIC)
- EconBiz
- Euromonitor Passport GMID
- Factiva
- General BusinessFile ASAP
- ISI Emerging Markets Information Service (EMIS)
- LexisNexis
- MarketLine Advantage
- OneSource Global Express
- ReferenceUSA

Strength Identification Resources

Institute of Character

The VIA Inventory of Strengths (commonly known as the VIA Survey) assesses strengths of character. VIA Survey-120 is a revised version of the original VIA-IS, which was developed by renowned psychologist, Christopher Peterson, PhD, as a 240-item, scientifically validated questionnaire that provided a rank order of an adult's twenty-four character strengths. The new revised version takes approximately fifteen minutes to complete and descriptive results reports are available for both individuals and professionals. Free survey.

www.viacharacter.org/SURVEYS.aspx

StrengthsFinder Assessment

To help people uncover their talents, Gallup introduced the first version of its online assessment, StrengthsFinder, in 2001, which ignited a global conversation and helped millions to discover their top five talents.

StrengthsFinder 2.0 is based on thirty-four themes and you can read this book in one sitting; you'll use it as a reference for decades. The assessment takes roughly thirty minutes and it's included in the price of the book. It will provide you with a customized report of your top five themes and how to articulate them.

www.strengths.gallup.com

Highlands Ability Battery

The Highlands Ability Battery is the gold standard among tools assessing human abilities or aptitudes. Developed from the pioneering clinical studies of Johnson O'Connor, it is a three-hour objective inquiry into the abilities and ability patterns of the individual who completes it.

The Battery consists of nineteen different work samples. Each work sample is timed to measure the speed with which the individual is able to do a particular series of similar tasks. The individual's score on each work sample establishes whether a particular task is more or less easy for that individual. Shown together on a personal profile and bar chart, the scores achieved by each individual reveal patterns or "clusters" of abilities that require analysis by a skilled interpreter. Once these patterns or "clusters" are understood, the individual is helped to guide his life and work into more productive and satisfying channels.

www.highlandsco.com/battery.php

The Battery may be accessed at www.abilitybattery.com.

The student website is: http://www.highlandsstudentcenter.com and the cost for the ability battery (plus two-hour "feedback conference") is approximately $200.

VALUES

A
Accomplishment
Achieving
Action-Oriented
Accuracy
Affection
Affluence
Appreciation
Ambition
Adventure
Altruism
Assertiveness
Attractiveness

B
Balance
Being the best
Belief
Beneficent
Balance
Beauty
Belonging
Bravery

C
Candid
Calmness
Camaraderie
Careful
Caring
Celebrity

Clarity
Coherence
Challenge
Choice
Collaboration
Commitment
Community
Compassion
Competitive
Connected
Control
Conviction
Cooperation
Creative
Credibility
Curiosity

D
Daring
Decisiveness
Dedicated
Depth
Dependable
Determined
Devotion
Dignity
Diligence
Directness
Discipline
Discovery
Discretion

Diversity
Drive
Durable
Duty
Dynamitic

E
Education
Efficient
Elegance
Empathy
Encouragement
Endurance
Energetic
Enthusiastic
Ethical
Equality
Excellence
Excitement
Expertise
Extravagance
Extroversion
Exuberance

F
Faithful
Fame
Family
Fascination
Fashion
Fearlessness
Fidelity
Finesse
Financial-independence

Fitness
Focus
Freedom
Forgiveness
Formidable
Free-Thinking
Frugality
Fun

G
Generous
Grace
Genuine
Gratitude
Growth

H
Happy
Harmony
Health
Heroism
Helpful
Honesty
Honorable
Hope

I
Imagination
Impactful
Independence
Informative
Intimacy
Inventiveness
Integrity

Intelligence
Innovative
Intuition

J
Joyful
Just

K
Kindness
Knowledge

L
Leadership
Learning
Legacy
Love
Logic
Loyal

M
Malleable
Mastery
Mindfulness
Meaningful
Memorable
Merciful
Modesty
Motivation
Mystery

N
Neat
Neighborly

Nimble
Noble
Nonconforming
Nurturing

O
Obedience
Objective
Openness
Opportunity
Optimistic
Organization
Original
Outstanding

P
Passion
Peace
Perfection
Performance
Perseverance
Persistent
Persuasiveness
Personal growth
Philanthropy
Pleasure
Popularity
Personable
Planning
Politeness
Positivity
Power
Practicality
Pragmatism

Privacy
Preparedness
Professionalism
Prosperity
Punctuality
Purity

R
Recognition
Relaxation
Resourceful
Reliability
Realism
Religion
Resilience
Resolution
Respect
Restraint
Routine
Romance
Risk-taking

S
Satisfaction
Security
Self-control
Self-expression
Sensitivity
Sexuality
Serenity
Service
Significance
Silliness

Simplicity
Solitude
Sophistication
Speed
Spirituality
Spontaneity
Stability
Strength
Structure
Success
Support
Surprise
Sympathy
Strength
Stability
Sturdy

T
Teamwork
Teaching
Timeliness
Tradition
Tranquility
Togetherness
Tough
Truth

U
Unity
Understanding
Uniqueness
Usefulness

V

Variety

Valiant

Vigor

Virtue

Vitality

W

Winning

Wisdom

Wealth

Wit

Y

Yes-minded

Youthful

Z

Zen

Zest for Life

STRENGTHS

Adaptability

Analytical thinking

Articulation

Authenticity

Building relationships

Communication

Conflict resolution

Creativity

Critical thinking

Curiosity

Decision making

Detail Orientation

Drawing

Emotional intelligence

Fairness

Focus

Foreign languages

Futuristic thinking

Goal orientation

Honesty

Humility

Humor

Imagination

Initiative taking

Innovation

Inspiration

Integrity

Judgment

Leadership

Learning

Listening

Making connections

Mathematical thinking

Negotiation

Networking

Optimism

Organization

Perseverance

Perspective

Persuasion

Photography

Planning

Problem solving

Project management

Public speaking

Results orientation

Sales

Self-assurance

Self-awareness

Self-discipline

Sign language

Singing

Story telling

Strategic thinking

Teaching

Training

Teamwork

Technical knowledge

Trouble-shooting

Video creation

Visualization

Website creation

Writing

ACTION VERBS

A
Accomplished
Achieved
Adapted
Addressed
Administered
Advanced
Advised
Analyzed
Arranged
Assembled
Assessed
Assisted
Attained
Audited
Authored

B
Budgeted

C
Calculated
Classified
Coached
Collected
Committed
Communicated
Compiled
Composed
Conducted

Consolidated
Constructed
Consulted
Contributed
Coordinated
Counseled
Created
Critiqued

D
Defined
Delegated
Delivered
Designed
Detected
Determined
Developed
Diagnosed
Directed
Discovered
Diversified

E
Earned
Edited
Eliminated
Encourage
Enhanced
Established
Estimated

Evaluated
Examined
Expanded
Experimented
Explained

F
Facilitated
Financed
Forecasted
Formulated
Fulfilled

G
Gathered
Generated
Grossed
Guided

H
Handled
Headed
Hypothesized

I
Identified
Illustrated
Implemented
Improved
Improvised
Increased
Influenced

Initiated
Inspected
Installed
Instituted
Instructed
Interpreted
Invented
Investigated

L
Launched
Lobbied

M
Maintained
Managed
Marketed
Maximized
Mediated
Modeled
Modernized
Monitored
Motivated

N
Negotiated

O
Observed
Obtained
Operated
Ordered

Organized
Originated
Overhauled
Oversaw

P
Participated
Performed
Persuaded
Pioneered
Planned
Prepared
Presented
Printed
Processed
Produced
Projected
Promoted
Proofread
Provided
Publicized
Published
Purchased
Pursued

Q
Quantified

R
Ranked
Received
Recommended

Reconciled
Recorded
Recruited
Redesigned
Reduced
Reengineered
Referred
Refined
Rehabilitated
Reorganized
Repaired
Reported
Represented
Researched
Resolved
Responded
Restored
Restructured
Retrieved
Reviewed
Revised

S
Scheduled
Secured
Selected
Solved
Spearheaded
Specified
Standardized
Strengthened
Structured

Studied
Summarized
Supervised
Supplied
Surveyed

T
Targeted
Taught
Tested
Trained
Transcended
Transcribed
Translated
Tutored

U
Unified
Upgraded
Utilized

V
Validated

W
Wrote

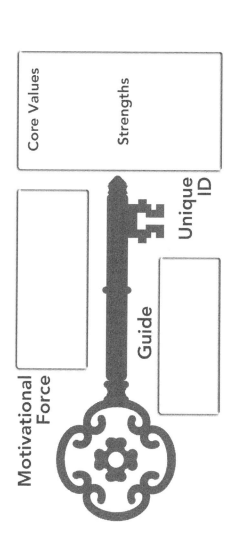

Core Values

Strengths

Motivational Force

Guide

Unique ID

ESSENTIAL BRAND STATEMENT

[1] Barclays Bank Delaware. "Miles of Possibilities: Bonjour." US Airways Dividend Miles MasterCard program. Accessed March 12, 2014. https://www.barclaycardus.com/apply/Landing.action?campaignId=1894&cellNumber=2&referrerid=PTRBA89FEE.

[2] American Express Company. "Power to Purchase. Power to Earn." Accessed March 12, 2014. https://www.americanexpress.com/us/small-business/credit-cards/business-gold-rewards/44279.

[3] Banana Republic. "Rewards are Always in Style." Accessed March 12, 2014. https://secure-bananarepublic.gap.com/profile/info.do?cid=7864.

[4] Amazon.com, Inc. "About Amazon." Accessed March 12, 2014. http://www.amazon.com/Careers-Homepage/b?ie=UTF8&node=239364011.

[5] Facebook, Inc. "About Facebook." Accessed March 12, 2014. https://www.facebook.com/facebook/info.

[6] Amazon.com, Inc. "Amazon Investor Relations." Accessed March 12, 2014. http://phx.corporate-ir.net/phoenix.zhtml?c=97664&p=irol-irhome.

[7] Constandse, Rodger. from "Time Thoughts Resources for Personal and Career Success." Accessed March 16, 2014. www.Timethoughts.com.

[8] McDonald's. "McDonald's Company Profile." Accessed March 12, 2014. http://www.aboutmcdonalds.com/mcd/investors/company_profile.html.

[9] Target Brands, Inc. "Mission & Vision." Accessed March 14, 2014. https://corporate.target.com/about/mission-values.

[10] Azadeh Ensha and Robert Moskowitz. "Tackle Out of Bounds Interview Questions by Rephrasing Them" and "Interview Tips—How To Handle Illegal or Out Of Bounds Questions—Part 1." April 12, 2011 quoted in "Employee Rights, Interviewing."

ABOUT THE AUTHORS

Dawn Ohaver Moyer is a Philadelphia University graduate, who has over twenty-three years' sales and marketing experience across varying industries, ranging from family-owned ventures to Fortune 500 companies. She is the recipient of multiple marketing and sales excellence awards, including two Effie Awards for advertising, and is widely recognized for her inspirational leadership skills.

Jenny Casagrande is a Temple University graduate who has over a decade's experience in marketing strategy, market research, and in-depth analytics in corporate America. She has two Marketing Excellence Awards and proven success in problem solving and shaping strategies to overcome complex business challenges.

Moyer and Casagrande are inspired by their participation in the launch of UN Women at the United Nations General Assembly and their roles as professional mentors with college programs and women's leadership organizations. They are the cofounders of Potential Essential, LLC, which helps individuals Discover their Potential and Become Essential.

For more information on Potential Essential, LLC, to schedule a workshop, speaking engagement or webinar go to www.potentialessential. com. Connect with us at:

https://www.facebook.com/discoverpotentialbecomeessential

https://www.linkedin.com/company/potential-essential-llc

Made in the USA
Charleston, SC
06 July 2014